TRANSITO

THE TRUTH BEHIND THE BIG-MONEY ROBBERIES

TRANSITO

THE TRUTH BEHIND THE BIG-MONEY ROBBERIES

Hennie Lochner with Peet van Staden

UNISA PRESS

Routledge
Taylor & Francis Group

LONDON AND NEW YORK

First published 2023
by Routledge
4 Park Square, Milton Park, Abingdon, Oxon OX14 4RN

and by Routledge
605 Third Avenue, New York, NY 10158

Routledge is an imprint of the Taylor & Francis Group, an informa business

Print edition not for sale in Africa

British Library Cataloguing-in-Publication Data
A catalogue record for this book is available from the British Library

ISBN: 9781032434476 (hbk)
ISBN: 9781032434483 (pbk)
ISBN: 9781003367376 (ebk)

DOI: 10.4324/9781003367376

Typeset in Delargo DTk
by UNISA Press, South Africa

UNISA university of south africa PRESS

CONTENTS

TABLES

FIGURES

PREFACE

By the time most people took in the relative ease, frequency and brutality with which massive amounts of money got taken, the phenomenon of cash-in-transit robberies had grown beyond the confines of mere South African crime.

It became the topic of fierce discussions on political and other public stages. Thousands of motorists were caught up in traffic almost every week when highways or other main roads were closed owing to such robberies. Rumours spread like wildfire and helped stir a media frenzy. Neither the companies moving the huge amounts nor the police seemed able to make any headway towards a solution. For some reason, they did not offer much information and this convinced many people that they did not understand what was happening or knew how to deal with it.

Clearly information was badly needed; frank and credible information. What information came forth, though, offered limited insight or sometimes caused more uncertainty. As usual, when insufficient information is available, people speculated and the urban legends grew. Random and superficial information simply would not do. Someone had to get to the source of the phenomenon and provide irrefutable findings.

Here, finally, is that information. As an academic and former police officer, it took one of us (Hennie Lochner) years of painstaking research as he had previously spent years investigating CIT robberies. The research was conducted according to the highest academic standards as part of doctoral studies. However, the focus remained on the practical problem of CIT robberies with a view to help police, security officials and criminal justice system to understand the modus operandi of perpetrators of CIT crimes and how to resolve these crimes swiftly.

Qualitative research methodology was used and interviews were conducted with the majority of convicted CIT robbers in this country. The duration of the interviews was 183 hours, producing almost a thousand transcribed pages of first-hand information. The process required not only exceptional probing, but also building rapport with the convicts.

This book is based on this research, but it is nothing like a thesis. It is intended for easy reading although it does not omit the detail required to understand the complexity this crime has attained. Both ordinary reader and student or security officer are taken on a journey of discovery into a fascinating world, first behind prison bars to meet the people who have no qualms to kill for big money. The often-asked questions are raised and answered fully and credibly: Who are these robbers? Why and how do they rob? What military training do they have? Why is CIT robbery so violent? Where do they acquire their firearms? What do they spend their millions on? What emerges is an inner circle of hardened, meticulous and clever elite criminals.

Other realities are also revealed. The need, method and dangers of moving vast amounts of money daily is visited and its flaws exposed. The police and their procedures are scrutinised along with the strengths and failings of their system. These are but two of several areas exploited by the criminals. The legal fraternity is another, and so are commercial establishments and civil entities from casinos and used-car dealers to sangomas who help robbers to evade the law and to launder their money.

Finally, the book reveals which well-established international investigative approaches have not been utilised, and what can be done now to loosen the grip on society of a threat that exceeds the boundaries of ordinary crime and seems to keep growing.

FOREWORD

Transito: The truth behind the big-möney robberies by Dr Hennie Lochner with Mr Peet van Staden comes at a time when cash-in-transit (CIT) robbery is showing another dramatic increase, both in frequency and ruthlessness. According to statistics annually released by the South African Police Service (SAPS), CIT robbery peaked in the 2006/07 financial year when the police recorded 467 incidents. As a result of the subsequent improved cooperation between the police and CIT companies, the number of incidents decreased year-on-year over the next decade to 137 in 2015/16, a decrease of 70,6 per cent. That seems to have been the turning point for what now appears to be developing into a new crisis. In 2016/17 CIT robbery already increased by 11 per cent to 152, and although the police's crime statistics for 2017/18 were were not yet available at the time of writing, all indications are that the rate of increase since then has intensified.

Within the cash movement industry there are huge concerns that unless something drastic is done soon, we may see a return to the high levels of a decade ago, or even worse. For example, Richard Phillips' joint chief executive of Cash Connect, in March 2018 already referred to the sharp increase in CIT robberies as "unprecedented". He was quoted in an IOL media report on 20 March 2018, titled "Cash spikes towards Easter", where he also cited the statistics for robberies affecting the CIT industry. According to Phillips the industry experienced a 43,3 per cent increase in armed robbery attacks from 256 in 2016 to 367 in 2017. Similarly, the South African Banking Risk Information Centre (SABRIC), in a press release on 13 March 2018, expressed "outrage" at the "brazen" CIT robbery earlier at OR Tambo International Airport. In 2016 SABRIC recorded 269 CIT robbery incidents compared to 249 in 2015, an increase of eight per cent at the time.[1]

Both Phillips and Kalyani Pillay, CEO of SABRIC, acknowledge that CIT robbery groups are highly organised and skilled. Phillips, in the media report of 20 March 2018, blames the new crisis largely on the failure by "law enforcement, crime intelligence and [the] criminal justice community" for what he terms "economic warfare" by organised gangs.

Lochner's book should be understood against this background. His research methodology allowed him not only to interview incarcerated CIT robbers serving lengthy prison sentences, but also, figuratively speaking, to get into their heads. In his book Lochner manages to combine absolutely revealing insights into the inner workings of CIT robbery groups with his many years' service in the SAPS as a detective investigating CIT robberies. The result is a meticulous and fascinating account of the nature and composition of these groups, also as individuals. It tells us how CIT robbery groups are formed, how they select their targets and how they plan and execute the attack (robbery). It also tells us about what happens after the robbery, how they escape, how they spend the stolen money, and why they often act with such complete disregard for human life.

For the general public this book will be hugely interesting as it provides an easy to read account of the activities of a specialised group of criminals who commit themselves to the robbing of millions of rands in broad daylight with the aid of stolen fast cars, explosives and sub-machineguns. This is a sub-category of aggravated robbery that is regularly reported on in the media, but about which very little otherwise is known. From time to time images of these crimes appear on social media or in the regular media, and on occasion members of the public find themselves unexpected witnesses. Some of the more daring onlookers even video tape such incidents without necessarily understanding the danger they put themselves in.

However, the real value of this book and the research it is based on, is the potential for actionable crime intelligence if properly utilised by the police and the CIT industry. Lochner succeeds in showing how this potential can be unlocked when approached correctly. He clearly shows how the modus operandi (MO) of these criminals can be determined and how it is possible to develop a profile of the groups and even the individual perpetrators. He highlights the professionalism with which they develop their plan for each robbery and the care they take with even the minutest detail.

With almost brutal efficiency Lochner exposes how the CIT criminals exploit the weaknesses within the criminal justice system and the CIT industry itself. He details how they bribe CIT and police officials, magistrates and prosecutors and how they use attorneys, fully aware of their criminal activities, to represent them. Even more shocking is the extent to which police officials actively participate in the provision of information, firearms and "safe houses". Much the same applies to CIT officials. The information in this book is so patently serious and alarming that the CIT industry, the criminal justice system and the entire legal fraternity must take cognisance of its contents and act on it.

The book closes with a range of recommendations relating to issues such as recruitment and training of CIT security officials. It also includes recommendations for the investigation of CIT robberies and the combating of these crimes in general. For that reason this book and its underlying research is regarded as invaluable for purposes such as the training of police detectives and CIT investigators alike.

Along with its general value, this book is a must read for all involved in the CIT industry, the police and the rest of the criminal justice system.

Dr Johan Burger, Senior Research Consultant

Justice and Violence Prevention Programme
Institute for Security Studies (ISS)
Pretoria

Note

1. SABRIC and Cash Connect use calendar years for their crime reports, compared to the SAPS' financial years, and also have slightly different definitions for what is regarded as cash-in-transit robberies.

ABBREVIATIONS

AK47	Russian designed assault rifle, officially known as Avtomat Kalashnikova
ANC	African National Congress
ATM	automated teller machine
BAL	ballistic
BMW	Bayerische Motoren Werke or in English Bavarian Motor Works
CAS	crime administration system
CCTV	closed-circuit television
CIT	cash-in-transit
FIFA	The Fédération Internationale de Football Association
IBS	integrated ballistic system
LDV	light delivery vehicle
MK	Umkhontho we Sizwe or uMkhonto weSizwe
MO	modus operandi
R4	South African assault rifle
R5	South African assault rifle
SAPS	South African Police Service
SARS	South African Revenue Services
ZANLA	Zimbabwe African National Liberation Army
ZAPU	Zimbabwe African People's Union
ZIPRA	Zimbabwe People's Revolutionary Army

INTO THE FACE OF VIOLENCE

> I walked to the accompanying vehicle where the cash-in-transit official was and shot the cash-in-transit official dead, because I wanted to be famous. ~ Participant 3 (Lochner, 2016)

The privatised correctional centre had all the trimmings of a maximum security prison. Its sterile terrain against the backdrop of the distant blue mountains and the luxuriant growth emphasised the high walls and the barbed wire fences.

Yet, once inside the new complex, it seemed different. Despite the obvious security measures, the grounds looked more like those of a high school. Prisoners from different blocks wore different coloured overalls. Inside the new building the floors were, of course, spotless in the bright lights radiating from the high ceilings.

This visit immediately created a favourable impression. The staff presented the biggest surprise. I was told on arrival that the prisoners were ready and waiting. All those I requested to interview, had agreed. Some others even volunteered. Other prisons had proved quite the opposite. At one prison I[1] was refused entry by a security guard despite elaborate prior arrangements. At another I was told that the lady with whom I had a confirmed appointment was out for the day.

The officer commanding turned out to have made the difference. His advanced academic background may have predisposed him kindly to the interviews I had requested. He clearly appreciated how important open doors are to a researcher.

I had driven a long way to interview five specific prisoners. All were convicted cash-in-transit (CIT) robbers. Some of them had killed. Most had committed other crimes for which they had never been charged. Some I had helped to get arrested, even if only indirectly. I was present during at least one of those arrests. Prior to this visit, I had also visited the scene of one of their heists.

The first CIT robbery took place at Phalaborwa before the term 'cash-in-transit heist' had even come into popular use. This heist involved a pick-up truck covered by a lightweight reinforced canopy which could hardly qualify as an armoured vehicle. It carried some tens of thousands of rands. At the time I warned CIT operators that they needed to be proactive, because very soon their people would be shot at.

As the tens of thousands became hundreds of thousands and later millions of rands, the CIT attacks became more frequent and more violent. The armour on the cash vans was enhanced. To stay ahead, the robbers became more sophisticated, their planning more precise, and the execution more lethal.

The one case that elevated the CIT phenomenon to a national outrage occurred towards the west of the then Northern Province, now Limpopo. The robbers struck in broad daylight on a summer's day, directly after a straight stretch of road between Potgietersrus (now Mokopane) and the little Bushveld hamlet of Tolwe.

As the police intelligence coordinator, I was responsible for the investigation. The investigating officer went to the crime scene immediately and I followed as soon as I could. As it turned out, I arrived some eight hours after the robbery. The crime scene had not been secured properly, exposing the lack of police experience at the sight of such unparalleled violence. It had been roped off but not yet released. Many people were allowed inside the secured area, some were sitting on their haunches sipping cold drinks. It became an example of how a crime scene should not be handled.

One of the security guards was still in his seat, shot dead and subsequently burnt out when the armoured vehicle was set alight. He had stood his ground protecting the R24 million in transit, earning his R11 000 a month salary.

A robber later told the police that the fire was an accident. For security, robbers would set themselves tight time limits, often leaving large amounts of money rather than exceed their allocated time. The robbers developed a tactic to slow the armoured vehicle down and then ram a heavy car into it to overturn it. This not only reduces the shooting options for the guards inside, but often disorientates and terrifies them. The idea is to get them to open the vehicle from inside before they regain their composure allowing the robbers enough time to take the cash. The armour on the vehicle easily withstands even rifle fire so cutting or breaking it open requires time – which they do not have.

Flashing a can of petrol while another robber with lighter in hand threatens to set the vehicle alight is designed to force the guards to open the door. Actually, setting it on fire destroys the money, which defeats the object of the robbery. The robber said his accomplice in this attack was not supposed to really strike the lighter, only to show it. But he did strike it – and the vehicle caught on fire.

The human cost of CIT robberies

Witnessing the results of such violence first-hand leaves its mark. Police members not only see the results but they are also exposed to the outrage and grief of the victims' relatives who come to court to hear how their loved ones were murdered. The police also become the focal point for demands for justice from the community. On the other hand, they hear robbers boasting of their actions – only to later deny guilt when appearing in court. The violence of CIT robberies is matched only by that of farm murders. Caught between the expectations of the victims and their families, and the defiance of the attackers, police officers occasionally face an unbearable test of their impartiality.

This has forced many police officers to do what I did – leave Limpopo for hopefully less troubled police pastures in Pretoria, but, like me, they eventually resign from the police force altogether. Only in my case, it did not stop me brooding about the nature of these attacks.

The questions about CIT heists remain. What makes the criminals capable of such levels of violence? Who are they? How do they work? How do they gain such influential contacts in such high places?

Even while commanding the Serious and Violent Crimes unit in the Northern Province, I had the habit of turning over my desk pad and scribbling random notes on different attacks, CIT heists and others. Revisiting the notes earned me the nickname of *Krappies*, (literally meaning a person who scratches or scribbles) because I never stopped scratching around for possible pointers. Certain trends and patterns emerged on re-reading those notes. Investigation and research require the same approach. You search and scratch, scribble notes and ask questions until you find the missing answer, which may not necessarily be the answer you want to hear.

These notes were put to some practical use during my involvement in the security industry following my resignation from the police service. I took many sheets of such notes along for the interview leading to my appointment as an academic. Those notes contained the nucleus of what would eventually become my doctorate on the topic. Much more work, of course, remained. That included the drawn-out process of seeking permission from authorities and the convicts themselves to do in-depth interviews with 21 people serving prison sentences for crimes related to CIT robberies. The convicts were serving their time in four of the long-term prisons in Gauteng, where most of the attacks had occurred. They represented most of the CIT convicts caught in recent years. Having eventually obtained the necessary permissions, I started the laborious process of asking each of them in a structured and scientific manner the many questions that had occupied my mind for all those years I was in the police service.

This process involved some eight hours of interviews per convict. I made a point of not selecting anyone whom I myself had arrested, although I had been present during some of the arrests. None knew or remembered me as a police officer.

After all, ten years had elapsed since some of those arrests took place. The arrests hit the suspects out of the blue, which is the intention. Police officers know that tackling CIT robbers is not child's play. The suspects are expected to be armed and dangerous. So, the police employ, as we did when arresting two of the Tolwe heist suspects in a house at Katlehong on the East Rand, a task force of some nine members. Such arrests are planned to take place between two and four in the morning, when even the dogs are asleep. The suspects are separated immediately.

Only then the search starts for evidence.

Demanding as the investigation and arrest usually are, they represent only half of the process. The other half is gathering evidence to secure a conviction.

As such, the place of arrest becomes an extension of the crime scene. The search needs to be as comprehensive as possible, because this is the one and only opportunity to secure evidence. I always insisted on physical evidence. Confessions are invariably disputed, drawing out the court proceedings. Some of the smallest items of evidence can have the greatest effect in solving a case. Everything can yield evidence: money and particularly paper strips around stacks of banknotes; ATM or fast-food slips could be solid proof of the whereabouts and numbers of a group; cars, shoes, gloves and other clothes yield DNA; while cellphones often reveal vital clues.

In fact, cellphone technology provided the key to solving the Tolwe heist. That, and the fact that one suspect cheated on his wife. She in turn revealed some of the information we needed. What we called 'pillow talk' yielded many valuable clues over the years.

Hearing from the robbers themselves

But that is history. Gathering methodical scientific information now presented a totally different challenge. The police officer had turned researcher. The search was no longer for evidence but for comprehensive data on a crime phenomenon that in some ways threatened society itself.

This book contains the inside data which my research yielded. In order to ensure ethical research practices were upheld, participants interviewed during the primary research phase were first consulted with and gave permission for the use of the information supplied, but usage is governed by strict conditions of anonymity. The identity of robbers and the names of the specific prisons where they were interviewed have been therefore withheld. Setting the theme per section, several chapters open with an anonymous but verbatim quote from one of the 21 convicted CIT robbers who were interviewed, and the same practice is followed with the detailed quotes provided within the chapters. For this reason, there will be no reference to the identities of the convicted robbers in all the chapters. All quotes are verbatim, in order to integrate the voices of the interviewees into the book's narrative while their actual words reflect the sometimes shocking reality of their opinions.

From the outset of the interview process, I made it quite clear that I was only researching the crimes for which they had been convicted. Nevertheless, virtually every convict was extremely suspicious. Some even refused to have their replies recorded. Once they realised that the information would not be used to incriminate them and their identities would be protected, they relented. One tried to intimidate me; others tried to impress. Some wanted sympathy. One convict told me that he'd been behind bars for 15 years and that he missed his children. I sympathised with him.

Some sessions had to be interrupted after an hour or so when a firearm was found in a prison cell or some other disturbance surfaced. With such an occurrence, all convicts had to be ordered back to their cells and the interviewing process had to be postponed to the next day.

Despite some interruptions, reluctance and even grandstanding, the process proceeded. Convicts came to trust me more and more. Details emerged of crimes totally unrelated to CIT robberies, including information about the body parts trade. Many revealed more about specific crimes than I asked for. They acknowledged carrying out several other crimes for which they had not been tried in court, including murder.

Some of those I interviewed about the murders they had been convicted of, denied direct intent, and instead provided other explanations such as:

> The intention was not to shoot.
>
> The intention was not to shoot to kill, but only to wound.
>
> The intention was not to shoot them but to deter them so that we can flee from the scene.
>
> The intention was not to shoot them but to damage their vehicles so that they could not follow.
>
> The intention was not to kill them but to intimidate them to follow our instructions.

One, however, was frank: 'I defeat them, and the only way to defeat them was to kill them, and in most cases to shoot them, because the chances to keep them under control are too slim.'

Another was even more radical: 'I walked to the accompanying vehicle where the cash-in-transit official was and shot the cash-in-transit official dead, because I wanted to be famous.'

Sometimes I couldn't help thinking: Skinny little *bliksem*! You are the most aggressive little scoundrel I have ever seen! How can you take someone's life to gain fame in crime? To advance in the hierarchy? But I knew that I needed to keep my opinions to myself, because I was a researcher, required to be impartial. And not only was I in a privileged position, I was also dependant on the interviewee for information.

Gradually a wider picture emerged revealing the involvement of the CIT robbery phenomenon in the greater society. This involved the role of police and women in the information chain of such robbers; the role of corrupt court officials, particularly prosecutors and lawyers, in thwarting the prosecution of robbers; the role of casinos, used-car dealers and lawyers in laundering the vast amounts of stolen money. In addition, robbers seemed to have a surprising ability to befriend female members from the ranks of university professors or lawyers and even buy them expensive gifts or property to please them or secure their silence.

The extent of CIT robbers' involvement in decision-making circles emerged through several seemingly unrelated incidents. One convict mentioned in passing that a well-known person would be arrested at the Comrades Marathon on a specific day. This predicted arrest happened in exactly that way.

In discussing the availability of information to convicted robbers, another boasted to me that he would be able to tell me the route that I would take to the prison when we had our next interview. For our next meeting I deliberately changed my route. True to his word, he not only knew exactly which route I had taken; he also was able to identify my car's model and colour.

Revealing and disturbing as this may be, my ultimate aim for interviewing the CIT robbers had an entirely different focus. I wanted to close in on a previously untapped information source for the more effective solving of the CIT puzzle.

Note

1. The use of the pronoun 'I' throughout the book refers to Hennie Lochner (the first author who conducted the PhD study upon which this book is based).

THE MODUS OPERANDI

A transgressor's modus operandi will always show the same recognisable actions, behaviour and patterns. ~ Labuschagne, 2015

Robbery is one of the most challenging crimes for law enforcement officials to deal with. Perpetrators come from all age, social, racial and gender categories – the only link being their need to acquire money or property illegally.

Robbery of businesses increased from 4 000 in 2006 to over 14 000 in 2009/2010 (SAPS Annual Report, 2011:14). Apart from the loss of property, robbery also causes fear (Berg & Horgan, 1998:242). More specifically, robbery with aggravating circumstances is one of South Africa's ever-increasing contact crimes. Incidents increased by 39,5 per cent from 101 039 in 2010/2011 to 140 956 in 2016/2017. CIT robberies are a sub-category of such robberies, and in many respects require the same investigation approach.

Crime investigators need information and evidence to identify a criminal. If no evidence is found at the crime scene or during the investigation, other methods are needed to find or generate such evidence. Two such methods are DNA analysis to individualise suspects or, for the purpose of this chapter, using modus operandi (MO) information to identify a perpetrator.

A crucial part of my research was to, for the first time in South Africa, establish the MO for such robberies as well as to build the profile of the perpetrators (Lochner, 2016). The research clearly revealed a profile containing an exceptional element of violence, combined with no respect for human life. The aspect of violence will be dealt with in some detail in the following chapters. This chapter focuses on the high value of establishing an MO, and on contextualising the crime of CIT robbery and the robbers themselves within the South African criminal investigation scene.

MO, as the Latin expression indicates, literally means a way of operating. Several researchers including Bell (2002) and Zinn (2007) suggest that as time goes by, criminals develop a set MO, reflective of their past successes and mistakes. Three phases of the MO can be identified: planning the crime, executing the crime and the behaviour or events afterwards.

Establishing the MO may be regarded as one of the legitimate methods for gathering information and as vital to uncovering the truth behind a crime. According to James and Nordby (2005:606), the concept first surfaced in American literature in 1654, although the term was used first in 1813 during a US patent law case when the Massachusetts circuit court presided over a dispute about an engine. Robert Heindel was the first person to record the MO of a transgressor and to use this during his investigation. He recorded, classified and analysed the actions of people who burgled houses in Germany (Fosdick, 1916:565). His sources of information were newspaper items, police reports and police interviews. He also interviewed burglars who were incarcerated at German correctional facilities.

Several researchers including Bartol and Bartol (2014:35), Brandl (2014:229-230), Fish, Miller and Braswell (2014:433) and Lochner, Horne and Zinn (in press) state that MO is the preferred actions and procedures used by a perpetrator to commit and complete a crime successfully. They add that these unique identifiable actions, methods and behaviour patterns develop as the perpetrator gains experience and feels more confident about the method used. Therefore, the elements making up an MO are unlikely to change dramatically over time. Berning and Masiloane (2012:84) see MO as unique learned behaviour, and this unique learned behaviour comprises the actions used to successfully complete a crime. Petherick (2009:299) echoes this viewpoint, although he argues his position from the perspective of a serial crime investigator. James, Nordby and Bell (2009:576), as well as Osterburg and Ward (2010:120) indicate that such learned methods and actions are the perpetrator's unique pattern of operation in preparing for and committing a crime and will provide a means of identification.

In their research, Bell (2002) and Zinn (2007) suggest that criminals in due course develop an MO based on their personal successes and mistakes. There are three identifiable phases to such modi, namely, planning the crime, executing the crime and behaviour or events afterwards.

MO in use for centuries

MO information has been recorded consistently in England since the late 1930s and used in crime investigation worldwide. According to Major (later Major General Sir) Llewellyn Atcherley, founder of the MO system, criminals follow a continuous, stereotypical pattern when committing a crime. They employ individualised techniques which can be recorded in a system as MO information.

MO information therefore is vital information about a criminal's actions and conduct during the three phases of crime. Usually this comprises visible evidence the criminal has left behind at the crime scene which was observed by victims, complainants and witnesses. The investigating officer records such information. Exclusive criminals, a category which includes CIT robbers and will be elaborated on later, usually get away from the crime scene leaving behind little or no MO information.

Most recent research suggests that such information may be objective or subjective, the source of the MO information determining its objectivity or subjectivity (Lochner, 2016:78, 265).

People such as victims, complainants or transgressors reveal subjective information. A transgressor's actions at the scene may be observed, conveyed or recorded subjectively. Subjectivity is due not only to the interpretation of witnesses, but also the subjective investigation of a crime scene and/or whether evidence is identified and documented.

Objective information denotes factual evidence or mute, indirect physical before circumstantial evidence. This is the physical evidence gathered at the crime scene itself. An example is spent cartridge cases or the combination of such cases identified and collected at the scene for analysis.

Currently MO information only covers crime execution

If during the investigation information surfaces about a suspect vehicle parked or used in the vicinity, those areas need to be investigated for physical evidence. From experience I know that criminals act carelessly, leaving valuable evidence such as cigarette buds or cold drink and fast-food containers. In my investigation of CIT robberies, I found slips for pre-paid airtime, automated teller machine (ATM) transactions and fast food purchases. One such a scene produced the cash slip from a hardware shop for the purchase of a cutting disc for an angle grinder used to cut open vehicles and safes.

Vehicles used by robbers may yield much physical evidence. Both the vehicle and its contents are considered as evidence. Those include entomological evidence in the form of insects. One investigation into targeted safes of agricultural co-operatives yielded drill bits in a vehicle. The rear end of one bit was forensically linked to the front end found in one of the safe doors at the scene of a crime.

Traditional MO information, which currently only covers the execution phase of a crime and is recorded accordingly, includes:

- The type of crime committed;
- The crime day, time and venue;
- The kind of property stolen;

- Characteristics of targeted victim;
- Roguery employed by the perpetrator;
- Pretence(s) offered by the perpetrator to gain access to the venue or premises;
- Other peculiarities displayed during the crime;
- The manner of the attack;
- The vehicle or preferred vehicle used;
- What the perpetrator said at the scene;
- The number of perpetrators at the scene;
- Routes leading to and from the scene;
- Previously compiled information and what was gathered at the scene;
- Methods employed to control victims at the scene; and
- The killing methods used.

Some researchers believe the quest for objective and subjective information should go further, for example to include the investigation and application of a transgressor's MO information. MO has been researched, but there is little information available on the application of an MO profile in crime investigation. Some researchers in South Africa have reported on MO information about bank robberies (Maree, 2008) and other incidences of robbery with aggravating circumstances, including CIT robberies (Thobane, 2014), car hijackings (Zinn, 2003) and household robberies (Zinn, 2007). Although international research is being done on the MO of CIT robberies, this chapter deals largely with the South African context.

MO as identifiable as fingerprints

Definitions of the term MO vary widely. Researchers such as Labuschagne (2015), Lochner (2016), Scott (1978) and Zinn (2007) regard it as a criminal's profile. They state that a transgressor's MO before, during or after a crime always consists of the same recognisable actions and behaviour, habits, patterns, acts, roguery, disguise techniques, secret languages or writing and other recognisable elements of this nature.

Researchers such as Scott (1978) argue that the perpetrator's profile is as recognisable as fingerprints and suggest that a robber can be identified as a suspect on the strength of this type of profile information.

In conducting my research, I concluded that criminals repeat certain behaviour (Lochner et al, in press). Becker (2009:173), Hess and Orthman (2010:7), James, Nordby and Bell (2009:714) and Zinn and Dintwe (2015:447) agree that the MO is how a criminal carries out a specific kind of crime, and according to Labuschagne

(2015:279) his signature may be regarded as what distinguishes the crime from other crimes or the criminal himself.

Marais and Van Rooyen (1990:67) suggest that a criminal's profile is constituted by his operational actions, roguery, disguise techniques, secret language, writing and signs. Becker (2009:281) takes a firm stand, declaring that MO can be as revealing as a criminal's profile. Gilbert (2007:178) acknowledges the fact that someone subjected to a tense situation will revert to familiar behaviour. Helfgott (2008:268–370) and Van der Watt (2015:177) however, state that should a suspect realise that he is under investigation, he will change his MO constantly.

Labuschagne (2015:278-280), a researcher and investigator of violent-crime, suggests that every crime has an MO by which the perpetrator may be identified. He calls it perpetrator identification, and it means the positive identification of someone who has committed a crime.

Should a criminal remain untraceable over a lengthy period, Brown (2001:116) proposes that the criminal may well be identified later on the basis of his MO since such a person usually follows the same pattern when repeating a specific crime.

It is disquieting to note the allegation by Axelrod and Antinozzi (2003:102) that most investigating officers regard the MO concept as simple and without practical use. Sennewald (1981:214) states succinctly in a definition that MO is nothing more than the 'method of operation'.

MO as court evidence

Kenny and More (2001:276) believe the ability to determine a suspect's MO may not solve the crime but it will indeed help to identify him. The identification of a suspect is sometimes achieved by determining how the crime was executed. This is referred to as the criminal's MO, and this is an important aspect for the investigating officer to consider when he wants to identify the criminal.

The more information available in a profile, the more accurate it becomes and the greater the probability that a suspect's profile will coincide with the recorded MO information. That is why most recent research recommends that convicted criminals should be interviewed and their profile characteristics be recorded (Lochner, 2016; Zinn, 2007, 2003). Compiling profiles and MO essentially enable investigators to use the information to identify criminals with certainty. Moreover, MO information can identify the connection between the perpetrator and the crime scene, or between the victim and the place where the crime was planned.

The information can also be used when investigating officers need to decide which types of evidence to look for at the crime scene, thereby affecting the division and allocation of investigation resources.

James and Nordby (2005:606) state that investigators and prosecutors use MO information to connect series of cases and to charge suspects in several cases simultaneously. It is also used successfully to corroborate or refute alibis. If it meets certain requirements MO information can be offered as evidence in court based on the doctrine of similar facts. Similar facts may be admissible in court provided there is a logical connection, known as nexus.

Identifying the perpetrator is complicated and controversial given the incidence of several wrongful identifications in the past owing to people's subjectivity. The traditional view is to collect and investigate all objective and subjective information so the perpetrator may be identified. Those include eyewitness accounts, personal descriptions, identity parades, recognition from photographs, voice recognition or MO.

Some researchers classify robbers as either professional or amateur, while others distinguish between long-term habitual or exclusive robbers, regular robbers and dangerous robbers. Measured by this yardstick, CIT robbers can be classified as exclusive robbers.

A small group of exclusive robbers

Marais (1989:47) suggests that only a small percentage of criminals are exclusive robbers. CIT robbers are exclusive robbers, but they represent a small percentage of all robbers.

My research findings indicate that there are only some 200 CIT robbers in South Africa (Lochner, 2016:135). Investigators can therefore ascertain from MO information that an exclusive robber was involved in a crime. The advantage is that the group of suspects becomes smaller.

The criminal careers of exclusive robbers cover at least one third of their lives. They rob when the risk of being identified is very limited and the financial reward is worthwhile. Their robberies are thoroughly planned and quickly executed. They act as a group and distribute tasks and responsibilities. They display excellent skills in handling vehicles and arms. Exclusive robbers do not hesitate to appoint, according to a predetermined business plan, professional robbers for specific tasks such as driving vehicles during a robbery.

Current research indicates that exclusive robbers show no respect for human lives (Lochner, Horne & van Wyk, 2018:223). What also sets exclusive robbers apart from other robbers is their ability to gather or develop information and to bribe officials in the criminal justice system. My research advanced substantive reasons why the profile of a sentenced CIT robber may most probably be regarded as the profile of a South African CIT robber (Lochner, 2016:267). One reason is that CIT robbers are not location bound: they carry out robberies across provincial boundaries. Also, the unique composition of robber groups means that a group never comprises the same members.

An outstanding characteristic of exclusive robbers is the planning of their actions before and after the crime. Such information is not normally part of MO information observed at a crime scene. It only emerges when sentenced transgressors are interviewed. Such information on the MO which was followed during the planning, execution and aftermath of the crime is valid.

Because this information is hard to come by, Zinn (2007, 2003) recommended that this method of compiling MO information be pursued continuously and under controlled circumstances. My own research came to the same conclusion (Lochner, 2016).

CIT robbers, as opposed to all other criminals, have an additional phase within their planning phase. In my research, I refer to this as the developing phase within the planning phase (Lochner, 2016:118). During this phase, the leader comes to the fore spontaneously and the different role players in the crime are identified. I also concluded that this phase enables CIT robbers to carry out their robberies successfully (Lochner, 2016:118). It shows strong similarities with the process the Police Service uses to gather information for the sole purpose of intelligence. It is known as the intelligence process.

Specialising to catch specialists

Crime investigation does not take place in a vacuum, and its success depends on the investigating officer's ability and preparedness to investigate cases to conclusion. Officers investigating CIT robberies have special skills and characteristics. Those include, although not their predominant skill, the ability to deal with all kinds of suspects under dangerous circumstances, as well as the ability to employ scientific investigation and interrogation methods. Those with strong analytical thinking skills would compile facts and other information, objective and subjective, for a three-fold purpose: to identify perpetrators, to locate them and to establish their guilt through facts, information and evidence. Such analytical thinking skills will also enable investigators to compile or have compiled overt and covert information.

CIT investigators also need the ability to work in a group context. This includes national investigating teams from the South African Police Service (SAPS) and the South African Revenue Service (Sars), investigators from CIT companies and private investigators. Irrespective of the point of view, all those have an investigating background, be it as former police members or from other institutions investigating crime or compiling information. They boast excellent informer networks and information sources.

Several investigating officers and researchers believe an MO file should contain two sections, one for information on crimes where no criminal has been identified and one containing information on identified, arrested and sentenced perpetrators. Researchers recommend that MO file revealed by sentenced criminals also be kept up to date in a file, because MO information on crime planning and the phase post execution is revealed either later or never (Lochner, 2016:297; Zinn, 2007, 2003).

To improve the effectiveness of police departments in the USA, the MO file is linked to other systems, particularly the one containing pictures of suspects and sentenced transgressors, known as the 'rogues gallery'. The use of such a combined system largely depends, according to Osterburg and Ward (2010:148), on how effectively the investigating officer adds the information he obtained from witnesses, collected at the scene or which was observed. The use and value of the file also depends on how the assigned officer arranges and splits up the information, and how that information will be withdrawn from it and disseminated. They suggest that the assigned officer is the ideal person to add new data. Palmiotto (2004:237) agrees, suggesting that the pictures should also be filed according to facial features and other unusual characteristics.

Becker (2009:279) states clearly that robbers specialise. They also develop a behaviour inventory of what worked for them in the past. They believe the behaviour they designed and applied in their careers will continue to be useful in future.

Who these robbers, particularly those involved in CIT crime, are and what shapes their behaviour will be discussed in the following chapters. Brown (2001:227) suggests investigators need to start their investigation by determining which of these actions and techniques the robber used before and during the robbery. In this manner, the trust a robber places in his tried and tested methods will become the investigator's greatest ally.

THE ULTIMATE CRIME

Criminals regard CIT robberies as the most prestigious crime because there is much money. - Participant 1 (Lochner, 2016)

Crime, particularly violent crime, has become a major feature of South African society. This phenomenon was fiercely debated in Parliament during a special parliamentary session in 2018. Crime statistics became a national obsession. The police came under intense pressure as they lacked the capacity to control the situation. In response to the growing crime rate, private security became a major industry, employing more people than the police service. According to Businesstech (2018), quoting SAPS data from 2017, 102 059 visible policing officers and 2,36 million visible private security officers were employed in South Africa.

Amid all other types of crime, two kinds began to dominate public interest – farm murders and CIT robberies. The prevalence of farm murders threatened the agricultural sector, the backbone of the South African economy and one of the major employers in South Africa. The other, CIT robberies, created a new organised crime industry, with the vast sums of money involved giving it something of an American prohibition gangster glamour.

These two crimes had one common denominator, namely the use of excessive violence. Even in South Africa, which has had its share of violence in the past, this was a shocking and sickening phenomenon. This chapter deals with the status of CIT robbers in South African crime, which partially explains the extreme violence they use.

Robbery is a street crime that has a strong psychological and social impact on society (Brandl, 2014:370; Osterburg & Ward, 2010:417). Not only victims, but their families and friends are also affected. This is also the reason why many people tend to lock themselves up inside their homes.

In its reporting protocols, the SAPS recognises seven categories of robbery with aggravating circumstances. One of the seven is CIT robberies. Yet South African law contains no definition of this specific crime. Suspects are instead charged with armed robbery. The CIT industry broadly define CIT robbery as the illegal and deliberate removal and appropriation of movable assets or cash by means of violence while such assets are under the control of the institution managing and handling them (Maree, 2008:1). Robbery with aggravating circumstances is described in legal terms as the theft of property by the illegal use of violence or threats of violence to convince the owner to relinquish an item or items (Joubert, 2013:149).

While such robberies have stabilised, their incidence remains unacceptably high in relation to the overall population in South Africa, and comparison with British and Australian statistics confirms this. Yet the most striking difference is the extent of the violence. Between 1989 and 2008, Australia had 89 reported cases, during which time no CIT staff member was injured. While South Africa's CIT crime-related statistics are somewhat obscure because of the uncertainty of statistics related to other associated violent crimes, nine officials were killed in the 2011/2012 financial year alone.

Between 2006 and 2007, CIT robberies in South Africa increased to 466 cases. An Institute for Security Studies researcher, Johan Burger, ascribes that to the closure of this country's specialised crime investigating units, including the Unit for Serious and Violent Crime (Burger, 2015). As a result of improved cooperation between the police and CIT companies, the next decade saw a 70,6 per cent decline in reported cases to 137 in 2015/2016. The prevalence had declined by 108 cases (23,2 per cent) in 2009/10, and then dropped sharply by 66,8 per cent or 239 cases in 2015/5. The average annual decline between 2006/7 and 2009/10 was 7,7 per cent, and between 2009/10 and 2014/15 it was13,4 per cent.

However, by 2016/2017, CIT robberies showed an increase of 11 per cent to 152, indicating a growing tendency. In total, South Africa experienced 3 088 reported cases of CIT robbery between 2004/2005 and 2014/2015. Even in the 'quietest' year, 2014/15, another 119 attacks occurred. Only the Northern Cape experienced hardly any attacks, with a maximum of four attacks occurring in the years mentioned. By way of comparison, Gauteng experienced 39 attacks, KwaZulu-Natal 18, the Western Cape 15 and Mpumalanga 14 within the 2014/2015 timeframe.

Table 1. The number of CIT robberies between 2009/2010 and 2018/2019

Year	Number of robberies
2009/2010	358
2010/2011	290
2011/2012	182
2012/2013	145
2013/2014	145
2014/2015	119
2015/2016	137
2016/2017	152
2017/2018	238
2018/2019	183

(Source: https://www.saps.gov.za/services/april_to_march2018_19_presentation.pdf)

The figures provided in Table 1 indicate that between 2009/2010 and 2018/19 South Africa experienced 1 949 reported cases of CIT robbery. This is considerably lower than the 3 088 cases reported between 2004/2005 and 2014/2015.

Billions in transit daily

It is impossible to indicate precise figures of the amount of money robbed during this process. Neither the CIT companies nor the police reveal the amounts which were in transit at the time of CIT robberies. This raises some uncomfortable questions. Would revealing the amounts affect the insurance premiums the CIT companies pay to their insurers should they carry more cash than their agreement stipulates? Or was the CIT vehicle not designed to carry as much? And somewhat cynically one may ask whether revealing the amount would affect the amount claimed from the insurance.

For the investigator, revealing the amount might yield a strategic advantage. Feeding the chronic suspicions among robbers about their final share as a portion of the initial take could only help solve such crimes more quickly, as will be pointed out in Chapter 20.

The CIT industry believes that cash transactions are the lifeblood of the economy, and cash in circulation is regarded as the veins feeding that blood into the vital economic organs. This exposes astronomical amounts of money to the risk of robbery. Different companies use vehicles designed to carry undisclosed amounts of money. This may vary between four and R60 million per trip.

Richard Phillips (2016), CEO of Cash Connect, believes the cash in daily circulation in the local economy to be approximately R130 billion. Some 90 per cent of transactions are paid in cash, which must be transported to banks and cash centres. Philips believes that CIT robberies impact heavily on trade, creating a shortage of cash for all transactions to the extent that the economy is effectively 'attacked' by robberies.

The loss of money is by no means the only concern. Phillips noted that no month passes without him attending the funeral of a CIT official. Either way, undoubtedly huge amounts of money are involved on a regular basis.

A closer look at CIT robbers, as interviewed

The 21 convicted criminals interviewed for this study represent some 75 per cent of all convicted CIT robbers in South Africa. One refused to have the interviews recorded, although what was written down after the interviews largely corroborated with the information provided by the others interviewed. Two other convicts wanted their information combined because they said they got married in jail. This explains the surface contradictions in some of the figures quoted here. All 21 convicted robbers were men. Although the ancillary role of women in CIT robberies would emerge as a notable feature, the name of only one woman convicted for CIT crime could be traced in the records. During the interviews, she was serving her time and has since been released. Nevertheless, the consistent referencing in this book to a robber as 'he' is offered as a generic term, and this does not exclude other genders.

Fifteen of the 21 robbers interviewed had an occupation at the time of their arrest, two of whom listed crime as their occupation. Both stated that they had been criminals from the start, never having done other work. Some of the others listed more than one occupation, which included the following:

- A bank official involved with financing motor vehicles who later had to ensure adequate cash for ATMs;
- A police officer involved with investigating crime;
- A CIT official employed by a company within the CIT industry;
- A taxi driver;
- The owner of a taxi business;
- A professional boxer;
- A business man supplying a telecommunications service to the public;
- A handyman with fixed employment whose main job was to cut shapes from steel using an acetylene torch;
- A businessman who would not reveal the nature or extent of his business;
- An entrepreneur; and
- A disco dancer.

The youngest, at the time of their first contact with the police, was 15 and the oldest 36, with the average age being 22. Many cut their teeth on petty theft, starting with bicycles and proceeding to cars. Often theft became robbery. One convict was 30 and working as a CIT official when he first had contact with the police. He shot a robber who tried to rob him while doing his job. He was charged with attempted murder. He claimed that the incident made him believe that justice was on the side of the criminal, leading him to take up crime.

Four of the participants would not reveal which crimes they had committed but which they had not been convicted of. It appeared as if they were cautious not to incriminate themselves. Some of the others may also have been deliberately evasive. One said:

> I am not sure about the amount, but it is quite a lot, especially the cash-in-transits ... and most of them we have done successfully even some of them were fake heist ... but most of them we were able to stop the car and take some cash boxes and run away with them successfully.

One of the participants who has never had a regular job, quantified his unpunished crime record as follows:

> I was arrested for car theft, housebreakings and once for fraud. I started to steal cars at the age of 15. I started to steal cars straight (parked vehicles). I have committed more than ... I would lie if I say it is less than 50 housebreakings. Cars forgot, I forgot, but it is thousand, thousands ... the cars are something that I have done more than I have done house robbery. It is something that I have specialised in.

Another indicated that he robbed between 25 and 52 houses and was involved in 30 or 40 vehicle hijackings.

One in three a killer

Seven of the 21 current convicts had committed murder. They were responsible for the deaths of 18 CIT officials and one civilian. Their intimidation tactics varied from threatening the use of firearms to threatening the use of petrol to set fire to the vehicle, and on one occasion, using a poisonous snake.

They acted equally violently towards accomplices or those they distrusted. Such people are often isolated in the criminal world. But what is notable is that CIT robbers will not hesitate to kill suspects. This distinguishes them from all other robbers.

CIT robbery is no spur of the moment crime. Such robberies are planned in minute detail. This alone establishes robbers as professional criminals. While many love showing off their money, they often display cautious behaviour, including maintaining day jobs, families and sobriety, particularly during robberies.

They gather information themselves by observation and enquiry although they often also use insiders. Their observation is focused and detailed, including how guards handle their arms and looking out for possible distractions. This is often supported by other observers, including women.

CIT robbers establish gangs based on the numbers and skills required for a specific robbery. This would include specialist drivers, accurate shooters, cutting-tool handlers and robbers who can handle diversions, the public and traffic. Such skills are drawn from experienced people, whose experience level is matched with the scope of a robbery. No member is recruited unless he has an established criminal track record or has been vouched for by another member. The gang is dissolved once the robbery takes place. Leadership is organic, temporary and not autocratic.

Robbers are mobile and do not limit themselves to one area, one province or even to this country only. Yet for an unknown reason no robberies took place in the Northern Cape, they occurred in all the other provinces even though most of the robbers themselves lived in Gauteng. Two of the robbers even struck in neighbouring countries. All the convicts interviewed took part in CIT robberies in every province but the Northern Cape. Most of the attacks were in Gauteng, followed by KwaZulu-Natal and North West.

The meticulous planning is followed by equally conscientious execution. This does not only enable the robbers to conclude a successful heist, it is also intended to introduce measures to avoid identification and arrest. Again, such an approach distinguishes the amateur from the professional criminal.

They wanted more

My research led me to the conclusion that the average CIT robber would probably be an experienced and professional criminal in his middle thirties with an extended history of violent crime.

Most of them had some income from regular jobs. So, the financial need could not have been that acute. The pursuit of a certain lifestyle, the example of friends or the demands of family members played a substantial role in drawing them into CIT robberies.

One robber stated simply: 'My taxi income wasn't enough. I wanted to improve my standard of living. Life is expensive out there.'

One of the participants explained at length his reasons for switching from other crimes to CIT robberies. The gist of this was that the crimes he had been involved with only enriched other people in the crime chain. His yield had been inadequate, so he took up CIT robberies because it involved greater financial gain. His explanation in his own words illustrates the type of thinking involved and reflects the other crime activities of a CIT robber:

> The reason why - with cars, I have seen it - that I am making somebody else richer. Because let us take for example I get [steal] a car that it sells for ... I sell the car for R20 000. Let us say we are two or three. We must divide the money equally. We all get five thousand and I know the guy who will take the car to Mozambique will sell it for R120 000.

After petty crime, some of them started doing cross-pavement robberies, where guards are attacked while they deliver or pick up money. One robber described grabbing such a box or trunk of money as 'a starter pack. You grab and run.'

Soon enough the potentially bigger gain swung the choice. Planning for a cross-pavement or CIT attack is, according to one convict, the same. 'The risk is the same, but the money is more.' Another noted that much money was available: 'going for it in abundance; that was the reason precisely.' One other convict noted the advantage of robbing cash instead of goods was that goods have to be converted into cash afterwards: 'There is much money. It is cash. That's why I like it.'

Another said: 'It is an easy crime to commit although they [the guards] are armed.'

One convict explained that a CIT robber has what he called:

> that mind of graduation - going to the next level - you see that the one you was doing is a petty crime ... want to do something that is bigger than what you used to do - motivation to get more millions easily in one day instead of making thousands.

So, the greed motive grows. The large amounts available feed that greed. As one convicted robber put it: 'Where there is money there will always be greed.'

Several participants regarded the shift to CIT robberies as a natural progression:

> In life of being a criminal you graduate from small or petty crimes to bigger ones.
> You cannot keep on doing small things.
> So, what I can say is that it was through experience and graduation in life that I have changed to cash-in-transit robberies.
> It was progression from normal robbery to cash-in-transit robbery.

Money breeds status. Greed breeds ambition and the results of fulfilled ambition create status. Someone who is able to spend large amounts of money, quickly gains status in the community. This does not only draw more recruits to crime; it also adds to the status of criminals. Even in prison, CIT robbers enjoy higher status than other criminals.

One participant boasted that he progressed to the point that other CIT robbers regarded him as the number one robber. He quoted news reports on the topic. I followed up on this information and it was verified.

One robber stated: 'Other people see you as below them if you are doing petty crimes.'

Another said: 'Criminals see the ability in you and they evaluate you according to the crime you have committed.'

Three participants believed that criminals are classified into three categories among themselves based on the kind of crime they commit. The more violent and profitable the crime, the higher the perpetrator rises in the hierarchy. The three regarded CIT robbers as being at the summit of the imaginary hierarchy.

One put this down to the amounts of money involved. Another stated:

> To commit cash-in-transit is the ultimate crime and you have been categorised. I have been recognised in my ability to do serious crimes and that is the reason why I have been selected to be part of cash-in-transit robberies.

A convict even indicated that because CIT robbers knew how much money was transported in an armed vehicle and therefore what their own share was likely to be, they acquired credit in advance.

Plans for some even more ambitious robberies emerged from the interviews. One robber said: 'A big job ... I think 200 million can be oraait [alright].'

A plan was hitched for an attack at OR Tambo International Airport. An attack group of 60 was formed. Among the group members they had 30 AK47s. (An AK47 is a Russian designed assault rifle, officially known as Avtomat Kalashnikova.) The target was, according to an informer employed by a security company, R100 million in foreign currency.

Those interviewed expressed a common conviction that suspects in CIT robberies have a lesser chance of being identified by the police or by witnesses. They based their argument on the fact that the gains from other similar crimes first had to be turned into cash. This aggravated the possibility of identification and arrest because those selling the stolen goods could be identified.

Selecting only 'really brave' members

While not one of the 21 convicted robbers had a tertiary qualification at the time of their arrest, criminals regard those who do CIT robberies as 'learned'. A convict said: "they know the system. We obtain information about the investigation of the CIT from the SAP (police members) who live with us in our area. We also have a police radio."

Two other factors may also contribute towards their status: the care they take in the composition of their groups and their treatment of sell-outs.

Beyond the previously mentioned considerations of experience, skills and personal connections, care is taken with the selection of gang members. A robber pointed out that they 'don't just pick. We must be sure of the individual's skills and how brave' that person is. A candidate might be trained, but not be brave enough. The choice for the group is simply: 'somebody who is really brave, somebody who can fight.'

More than one participant indicated a suspicion of candidates from KwaZulu-Natal despite some links with the province among those interviewed. An acknowledged leader who, by his own admission, committed most of his CIT robberies on the West Rand, mentioned that he did not accept robbers from KwaZulu-Natal into his groups. His controversial reason is that they shoot randomly, were aggressive and that in his opinion the police paid more attention to cases where there was shooting or where bystanders or CIT officials were killed or wounded.

His position coincided with another's view that when only 'two' spent cartridge cases are found at the scene it indicates that professional robbers were involved. But 'if more than 26 spent cases are picked up, they were Zulus'. He elaborated: 'If there are Zulus at the scene, it rains bullets. They shoot to kill.'

The dominant language among them may have been isiZulu (see next chapter), but only two grew up in KwaZulu-Natal and none lived there at the time of committing the crimes that they were convicted for.

Suspect gang members 'must go forever'

The veteran of West Rand robberies quoted above gave an estimate which would seem to emphasise the position that robbers are recruited from well-known or existing groups. He said he was aware of some 200 CIT robbers in the West Rand-Johannesburg-Pretoria area. According to his indication, only 14 were from Johannesburg and 28 from Pretoria, meaning the West Rand had 158.

Once a member becomes suspect, the reaction would depend on several considerations and circumstances. Isolating him from the crime community has already been indicated as an option, but more drastic steps are possible. 'We might take him out. That means he must go forever. He must die. He is not good. We as the group will take him out,' one robber said.

It might happen at the scene of a CIT robbery or elsewhere, depending on safety and other strategic considerations.

One robber admitted killing some of his friends because they were suspected by the group of having 'pimped' on them, as he put it. 'I was very sad because I shot them, and then I attended the funeral.'

In the final analysis, CIT robbers seek personal financial gain only. 'I wouldn't call us syndicates. We get together, plan, do what we have to do and disperse, one robber said.

That said, many questions remain about these robbers, including their origins, education levels and the popular assumption that they have undergone military training. The next chapter examines those topics.

WHO ARE THESE ROBBERS?

> You also want to live the same life. You follow them and do what they do. ~ Participant 1 (Lochner, 2016)

Despite some speculation in the media[1] at the time, the latest research contradicts the notion of some military 'third force' with a political agenda carrying out CIT robberies. In fact, no political or other aim beyond personal greed came to the fore during my research. Whatever motive there may or may not have been, this chapter confirms that the perpetrators had very limited military training.

Only one robber had received specialist training. He underwent training in the former Communist Bloc as a freedom fighter and was involved in actual shootings during the struggle for democracy in what was then called Rhodesia, now Zimbabwe (Lochner, 2016:88). Another received some training in the use of firearms as a CIT official.

Seven of them were single and five married. Four got divorced while in jail, and the spouses of two others died while their husbands served their sentences. All had children. Seven of them grew up with their grandparents, the others with their parents.

One of the two who grew up in KwaZulu-Natal would not specify where. The other one came from Newcastle. The rest were born in Gauteng, except for one who was from Limpopo and the Zimbabwean who hailed from Matabeleland. Two were from Soshanguve and another from Sunnyside in Pretoria. Tembisa produced two and a third came from nearby Springs. One was born at Heidelberg in south-eastern Gauteng. Two came from Alexandra and five from Soweto, three specifying Kliptown, Orlando and Dobsonville.

Thirteen of them had moved from their place of birth by the time they committed the crimes they were sentenced for. Although there were some differences of opinion, 12 listed as high crime areas the places where they lived at the time of the crimes. At that time, the Zimbabwean was living in Sandton. A second convict merely stated different towns in different provinces. Three were from Soweto of whom one specified Dobsonville. Another three lived in Johannesburg, with high-density Hillbrow being specified by two of them. Two lived in Soshanguve, two in Mabopane, and one in an unspecified part of Pretoria. One each lived in Alberton, Brakpan, Kagiso, Katlehong and Tembisa.

Of the 21 people who were interviewed, eight were isiZulu speakers. Three spoke Sesotho (Southern Sotho), three Setswana and one each Sepedi (Northern Sotho), isiNdebele, siSwati and Afrikaans.

Friends and lifestyle were their two main reasons for getting involved in CIT robberies. One robber explained the influence his friends had on him:

> The lifestyle is different to yours. You also want to emulate them. Trying to follow what they are doing and how they are living. You also want to live the same life. You follow them and do what they do.

Some had friends who were already into crime, and one was, by his own admission, gradually introduced to CIT robbery.

Another recalled:

> It is like an attraction and also the friends that you meet. Friends were already involved in cash-in-transit or other robberies, not specifically cash-in-transit robberies but in other robberies ... and I was influenced to be part.

Several told similar stories:

> I was sitting with another guy who did program me that cash-in-transit can give you too much money.

> Some influence because of the guys I associated with. I want to be like them and not like somebody else.

> *Ek het 'n groot plot gehad. Die medebeskuldigdes het gereeld daar kom beplan. Hulle het daar kom drink en my beïnvloed met baie kontant wat hulle by hulle gehad het. Beplanning is hier gedoen. Hulle het gesê hulle gaan die kontant-in-transito-trok vang.* (I had a large plot. The co-accused went there regularly to plan. They came to drink and influenced me through the abundant cash they had on them. Planning was done there. They said they were going to catch a cash-in-transit truck.)

Pressure of friends and money

Another participant mentioned that financial pressure caught up with him because he got used to the crime and the financial gain of other CIT robberies. He described the financial pressure as follows:

> I get 900 000 ... then that is much. Let me put it this way: greed. I wanted to have more cars, girlfriends and their lifestyle was changing, we started to change our lifestyle, clothing and fancy things ... and I wanted more cars and more money.

One enrolled his children in a private school and identified the financial pressure of keeping his children in that school as a reason for participating in CIT robberies.

While no one pointed out tertiary education for their children as a motive for CIT robbery, seven of the participants indicated that they contributed financially towards their children's studies. One mentioned proudly that his child was studying in the Netherlands courtesy of money stolen during CIT robberies.

Sixteen of the participants passed Grade 12 at school. As indicated before, none had tertiary qualifications while doing crime although two had enrolled at Unisa. Both completed their qualifications after sentencing. One of them was in the process of furthering his studies and he was going to be utilised by Correctional Services to provide computer training to fellow convicts.

One of the participants who did not complete Grade 12 at school did so after sentencing. He also obtained a marketing management diploma and an N6 qualification in business management.

Two others were enrolled at Unisa when interviewed. Both were in their third year. Another mentioned that he had started on a master's degree in education which he dropped in 2013 owing to what he called a lack of communication with his promoter and problems with his test sample.

Some mentioned a link between employment and a suitable qualification. It would seem they were improving their qualifications with a view to obtain better employment opportunities after release. It emerged from the interviews that all those sentenced to life imprisonment participated in the internal training programmes offered by Correctional Services.

The deadly consequences of their greed

The SAPS recording and reporting of CIT robberies as well as murder cases make it impossible to ascertain exactly how many people died during CIT attacks. However, from the interviews it emerged that CIT officials died in all the cases covered in this research except one where a passing motorist was killed by a stray bullet. CIT officials died in two other cases, but the perpetrators were not sentenced to life imprisonment. In all, seven participants were responsible for the deaths of 18 CIT officials and one civilian.

Two were caught red-handed through proactive police action. A third was wounded by a CIT official and arrested at the crime scene. The rest fled and were only arrested later. They shared their suspicions about the possible reasons for their arrest:

- Good cooperation between the police and CIT company investigators. Most participants suggested that the investigators were former police officials;
- Information supplied to the officials by former female or male friends;
- Information supplied by eyewitnesses on the scene that led to the identification of vehicles used in the robbery;
- The use of cellphone technology by the police;
- Information supplied to the police by accomplices during arrest and interrogation;
- Anonymous information supplied by accomplices who believed that they were cheated when the yield was split;
- Information supplied by informers following rewards being offered;
- In the opinion of one convict, he was arrested through an agent who penetrated their group. He based his statement on the fact that all but one were arrested;
- SAPS investigations once reckless spending and the purchase of luxury vehicles were brought to their attention;
- Information supplied to the police by competing CIT robbers; and
- Two believed they were caught in a trap.

However, the analysis of information from the interviews suggested a somewhat different set of reasons:

- Fingerprints left on vehicles at the crime scene;
- DNA in the form of blood at the scene owing to crashes or bullet wounds;
- Evidence by co-accused offered in terms of Section 204 of the Criminal Procedure Act (which deals with incriminating evidence by a witness for prosecution);
- Ballistic evidence from firearms found in the possession of suspects or co-accused;
- The use of cellphone technology to determine locality and movement;

- CCTV footage; and
- Seven participants mentioned that the confessions they made to magistrates were used against them. One called it the worst mistake he made and regarded it as having led to his convictions. It was, he said, 'a very stupid thing to do'.

A detailed crime history

This information suggested that investigating officers made ample use of the provisions of Sections 204 and 205 of the Criminal Procedure Act. These sections allow investigating officers to use certain circumstantial evidence as evidence and to acquire evidence from cellphone companies, for example.

According to the versions provided by the participants themselves, a difference could be detected between what they believe led to their arrest and the facts offered as evidence during their conviction.

Nine had other prior convictions, three of whom had been found guilty of more than one crime. Nobody mentioned being convicted for the same crime twice. Two of the nine were convicted for theft, two for car theft and hijacking, and one each for armed robbery of a fast-food outlet, assault, fraud, hijacking a truck, housebreaking and theft, house robbery, robbery, robbery of a pay-out point and theft.

The sentences they were serving for CIT-related crime was evident from both the interviews and the admission documents that all convicted criminals in correctional facilities are compelled to carry on them all the time. Four of them were tried together in one trial and convicted for two different CIT robberies. The charges included six for murder and two for CIT robbery.

These are all the crimes they were convicted of:

- Attempted murder;
- Escape;
- Illegal possession of arms and ammunition;
- Murder;
- Robbery;
- Robbery with aggravating circumstances (including three where eyewitnesses were robbed of their vehicles at the crime scene); and
- Theft.

Some of these men also revealed involvement with other crimes disregarded in this research. These include driving under the influence of liquor or a drug with narcotic effect, trespassing and crimes related to formerly illegal political activities under security legislation applicable at the time.

One mentioned that he became involved in the habit-forming drug trade while on the run from the police for the CIT robbery for which he was imprisoned. His rationale for the switch was that the crime received less attention from the police than CIT robbery with a resultant smaller chance of being arrested. He called it 'easy money'.

Four of the convicts were sentenced to life imprisonment (25 years before being considered for parole) six times. One was given two life sentences. Another was sentenced to life imprisonment.

Excluding the life sentences, 11 CIT robbers were sentenced to an average of 28,8 years. The lightest sentence was 13 years, another got 18 years, two got 20 years, two got 25 years, one got 28 years, one got 32 years, one got 38 years, one got 48 years and the final one was sentenced to 50 years.

Research established the average age of these convicted robbers as being 35 years and 5 months. This should, however, not be regarded as the average age for active CIT robbers since 14 of them indicated that they had been involved in prior robberies for which they were not arrested.

All but four of the interviewees also robbed CIT guards who delivered or collected money from businesses. Three of the 14 said they had been arrested for prior CIT robberies, but that the charges were withdrawn.

One convict mentioned that he was found not guilty on a prior CIT charge. Another had already been sentenced for a previous CIT robbery and was out on parole when he became involved in subsequent robberies for which he was jailed.

Faster results require broader strategies

Five CIT robbers interviewed were arrested within a year of committing their robberies. Eight got arrested within two years and one was arrested within the third year, but for a different crime:

> I was arrested by other people, by other department, by other officers because I had about two big escapes cases. When all these cases of Cape Town, Pretoria, Johannesburg were combined, I had about 12 cases.

The research suggested it had taken so long to trace the suspects because they had not returned to their own well-known addresses or haunts. Neither had they returned to the homes of family members or areas regularly raided by the police.

The research also convinced me, given my experience in investigation, that a group of SAPS and CIT company investigators adept in a variety of fields would have achieved better results. An investigation team should ideally include experienced people in fields such as financial or vehicle investigation. This enables the team to broaden their investigation with regard to fixed and moveable assets.

One of the problems with identifying CIT robbers is that some try to blend into normal society. The profiles produced from this research data will provide more in-depth insight into criminals, their place in society before and after their crimes, and how they go about avoiding prosecution. The research also reveals information about the reasons and motives for committing crimes, and why CIT robbers become involved in that crime.

This information on CIT robber profiles will enable crime agencies to recruit informers in the right places. It will also guide investigators to focus on which areas, places and people to deploy informers to in order to solicit specific information. Such information could aid policymakers with proactive and retroactive SAPS action.

Of equal importance is knowing who leads robber gangs and what planning goes into those attacks, which are the topics of the next chapter.

Note

1. See https://www.iol.co.za/news/south-africa/the-anatomy-of-a-cash-van-heist-114984

PLANNING A CIT ROBBERY

> We give him that respect; he is the mastermind. We give him that honour. We call him a kingpin. ~ Participant 9 (Lochner, 2016)

There are essentially two methods of executing a CIT robbery. The one is forcing a moving CIT vehicle to a stop, using a variety of methods; the other is robbing the CIT guards while they pick up or deliver cash and their vehicle is stationary, the so-called 'cross-pavement robbery'. There is little difference between the two methods because the planning is very similar. The interviews with the convicted CIT robbers confirmed the similarities, and I agree, based on my experience of CIT investigation. This chapter examines the meticulous planning process that goes into a CIT robbery and explains the unusual concept of gang leadership.

The robbery is an entire project on its own, starting spontaneously as a new idea, not as a result of a post mortem of a previous project. It is developed entirely on an individual robber's own initiative and essentially involves obtaining information.

The following information is gathered:

- Locating and observing an operational vehicle from a CIT company collecting or delivering cash for clients or businesses, including those that replenish ATMs;
- Observing the premises of a CIT company to gauge the movement and deployment of vehicles and manpower;
- The movement of CIT employees on or off duty. The aim is to identify workers who may be approached for information. Shebeens, premises broadcasting sport or liquor outlets have been identified as such places; and

- Filling stations close to CIT company premises are also watched to identify employees who buy fuel. Three participants mentioned looking how much fuel those employees put in their cars. The less fuel, the greater the possibility that the employee could be in financial trouble and the more susceptible he or she may be to supplying information.

The CIT companies and their employees are not the only ones targeted; the employees of their clients are also watched. The aim is to find out the times when the money is delivered or picked up, how much is involved and what security measures are in place.

An insider – an employee who has already supplied information leading to a successful robbery – may be approached again to supply or confirm new information.

CIT employees identified as possible sources of information are approached subtly and gradually corrupted. The corruption process is sustained and repeated until, in the opinion of the majority of participants, adequate information has been compiled to set up a meeting with a potential group of robbers.

Information is also exchanged with established CIT robbers who have a good track record. One participant explained it as follows: 'A job comes to your attention because of previous experience.' This is another reason why groups for subsequent CIT robberies are constituted in a dynamic and unique way for every robbery.

The first meeting, once a potential target has been identified and adequate information has been compiled, is no structured affair. Arrangements are made by cellphone.

However, participants were not clear about who attended such meetings, except that those present would be the ones who generated the information. Asked if all members of a group attended every planning phase, one participant said:

> In the preliminary stages you may find that all members are not around. Some might be having some excuses because it is not knowing exactly what is being brought … In the second stage you know exactly. We know all the members that are supposed to be there, but preliminary … in the first instances you get five, six or seven of the people and then everybody will say so and so is coming.

Those interviewed also pointed out that no CIT robber would attend the first meeting without having participated in a successful robbery. The reason offered was that he could make no contribution since he had no experience. Subsequent meetings would take place as facts and information are followed up and further planning is done.

From the interviews, I gathered that every meeting, from the first to the last, involves primarily verifying information and formulating action plans for executing the robbery. The number of meetings held varies according to three convicts.

> Depending on what is needed to be discussed, this thing - the planning - takes some time and it moves in stages to stages up until to the final day of the consignment.
> Sometimes you do it (meet) once or twice a day depending on the planning.
> Many stages and meetings until commencement of operation.

Two group members who regarded themselves as professional robbers mentioned that they met over a long period and that it could take months to check and verify all the facts.

The venue for the first meeting is determined summarily via cellphone to ensure that only the necessary people attend. It is also done to protect the information acquired and to ensure that it does not leak out.

No distinction is made between the venue for the first and subsequent meetings. One member did mention that they were cautious about using the same venue because they worried about the group becoming infiltrated and the police installing eavesdropping devices or cameras. Several venues were mentioned for meetings where preplanning was done:

- At the residence – townhouses or apartments – of one member, primarily that of the person regarding himself as leader and acting accordingly;
- In the open veld in one of the former homelands. One of the robberies was carried out there;
- At the lodge of one of the co-robbers;
- On a smallholding belonging to one of the members who operated a shebeen there;
- Different premises, including public parks in Johannesburg, Kagiso, Soweto and Pretoria; and
- At several filling stations and fast-food restaurants in Midrand.

An analysis of the responses showed open spaces to be the favoured rendezvous because other activities or people could be observed from a distance. Such spaces also lessened the threat of eavesdropping.

From this I concluded that robbers are always alert not to draw attention or create suspicion. Some robbers pointed out the dangers of holding meetings in the homes of group members, saying this created suspicion among family or friends. Also, when police investigate a CIT robbery involving family members, those people are sometimes subjected to thorough questioning and on occasion are held as suspects. Neighbours might sometimes smell a rat and supply information on vehicles or descriptions of people to the police before or after the robbery. Several vehicles in one place might also raise the suspicion of police members on patrol.

First there must be a job

The development phase of a robbery involves carefully considering the action plans the robbers come up with, determining the risk, and laying the groundwork and carefully arguing the finer points about the execution. One key aspect is the precise and complex composition of the CIT robber group, and the individual and group duties during the planning.

Topics under discussion include measures for the selection of group members, considerations when executing a CIT robbery and methods of gaining information on the intended CIT company.

The planning phase only follows the developmental phase once adequate information has been compiled for the intended robbery. Steps in the developmental phase may differ, but members meeting to plan a CIT robbery is the first step in the planning phase. From this meeting flows the organised tactical planning which comprises different facets.

The complete explanation by an experienced CIT robber who has planned and executed several successful CIT robberies struck me as typical of how the other interviewees see the origin of the first planning meetings:

> At first there must be a job (robbery project). The job must come with somebody. For me to call other people to say there is a job I must first verify that there is really a job to be done. If I am convinced that this guy is telling me the truth, it is where I start arranging other guys. If we find that this is right, we contact the others because you can't just see something alone and then you tell people that we are going to do this thing [planning].

Before the first meeting, a leader would emerge spontaneously to initiate the meeting. Several key role players would be invited to the meeting, but the remainder of the group would still have to be recruited. External factors directly influence the composition of the entire group.

The leader, as pointed out previously, would not be elected democratically. Instead he would become regarded as the leader naturally, sometimes by himself or a small number of the group. An analysis of the responses indicated that the leader is responsible for most tasks and decision-making, and is respected but not regarded as the 'boss'. However, there would never be a ballot for or the election of a leader. In some cases, more than one person acts as leader, but they do not function separately, and one does not take a decision without consulting the others.

Four of the participants indicated that they acted as leaders. Notable reasons were given for identifying themselves as leaders.

One suggested that he was regarded as a mainstay of the group:

> I don't want to mention myself, but there were three guys who were the [pillars] of the organisation. We were three in fact, but among the three nothing was going to take place if I was not around. I was important for disciplinary measure.

Another reasoned that he was the leader because he organised the information, firearms and stolen vehicles, and he was an excellent driver. The link he tried to establish between his driving skills and his leadership is unclear, however.

A third one said he did all the talking and gave instructions, and that trained *Umkhontho we Sizwe* (MK) fighters were prepared to accept his authority. No participant in this research was a member of MK, the disbanded former military wing of the ANC (African National Congress). Some former MK members were, however, part of CIT gangs.

Not a boss but a mastermind

From the replies by interviewees it became clear that the culture of not voting for a leader indicated that most members were already experienced. They respected each other for being seasoned project planners, and for their knowledge and ability to execute CIT robberies successfully. A second important consideration to emerge was the information a potential leader had or has compiled about the potential robbery. The knowledge and availability of firearms and robbers who have so-called special characteristics was a third important element, and the final one was that the leader should have participated in several successful CIT robberies.

Those who did not regard themselves as leaders listed their reasons for supporting someone else as leader. A good leader must:

- Maintain good discipline;
- Make all the arrangements;
- Gather all information about the possible robbery;
- Recruit the other group members;
- Make contact with people who could provide stolen vehicles;

- Have been involved in other newsworthy and successful CIT robberies; and
- Be the most experienced criminal in the group.

One participant called the leader the 'mastermind' behind the planning of the CIT robbery, which essentially sums up everyone's feelings:

> He is the mastermind. He is the one that organises everything - he runs the show, but he is not a boss to us; he is a man that we know is going to do brainstorming of the things and he comes most of the time with ideas of where we should get guns from, how many stolen cars do we need to make the robbery successful - the safe house and organising all those things. But most of time we have someone who is more like a leader, we give him that respect, he is the mastermind. We give him that honour. We call him a kingpin.

All the robbers interviewed confirmed that CIT planning was thorough. Discounting one who was recruited a day before the robbery, the participants spent no less than three weeks on planning. The longest was 14 months. In this instance, the robbery had initially been called off shortly before the execution phase because roadworks had started on the access route where the crime was supposed to take place. The robbery was postponed until the completion of the road works.

One participant referred to the planning stage as a 'research project', calling it the most interesting part of the entire robbery. A robber involved with many CIT robberies regarded it as the phase for drawing up the master plan.

One who was part of successful robberies beyond what he was convicted for, ascribed his arrest to poor planning:

> Yes, I was called to participate on the day of the robbery. Another reason why I say it was not properly planned: we only had one AK47. We are not supposed to have one AK47 in a robbery as big as this one, we should have four to five AK47s ... We had one AK47 and we had about four pistols ... so these pistols are not in a good condition. It could not shoot when I tried to pull the trigger. It did not shoot - there was something wrong with the gun. Those are some of the mistakes that I could say it was not properly planned.

Other participants added:

> You do not do cash-in-transit [robberies] without planning. These are important things you must consider: you have to plan the site. Scouting the place. It takes time. You must get information. You must be certain there is money. The area must be safe. The area is scouted nine times.
>
> I do not rush things. I did the planning nicely.

> Use a straight [registered] car which will take us to a safe place ... so most of the time it is more safe on the road than doing something inside a bank or inside a casino. So basically, that is why I was arrested: because the planning was not good.
>
> But there are people who are committing those kind of operations impulsively without planning. Which is not good, you know.
>
> The modus of operation is the one that you dwell intensively on. You drill over it. The drilling over this is precisely to perfect what you are doing.

Trusting one another is the key

Accomplices are incorporated into the group by the leader, on the recommendation of his confidants or for their special skills. The interviews revealed three important considerations for identifying and choosing accomplices. The first is trust, the second is the driving skill of the people tasked to bring the CIT vehicle to a stop and to drive the robbers from the scene afterwards, and the third is the handling of firearms at the scene.

The interviewees used the word trust 69 times to stress the importance of group composition and the choice of accomplices. It included the trust based on the leader's reputation for successful CIT robberies.

Other aspects of trust were that:

- A robber would not talk to outsiders about robberies;
- He would not reveal information to the police during interrogation;
- He would act fearlessly on the crime scene;
- He would not spend money recklessly;
- He would be prepared to act violently against co-robbers;
- Robbed money would be divided equally and not stolen beforehand; and
- He would always safeguard the identity of accomplices.

The view of one robber who identified himself as a leader may help investigators working on CIT robberies. His view was that CIT robbery was no breeding ground for novices:

> We never work like that in my game. I want people who have at least ... or who have the experience in robbery. If you are new, you have never done that - sorry.

One member, who identified himself as a leader, suggested that a group might work together again following an efficiently executed robbery. He said this happened rarely because mutual distrust always existed among members.

In my opinion, this is another point for investigators to consider. Distrust was often raised as a possibility when participants discussed how they came to be arrested. Several suspected their female companions of having revealed their identities. Distrust also emerged as a consideration in the distribution of and dealing with large amounts of cash.

Robbers tend to use one of two approaches when they suspect one of their own. They will quietly check his phone for signs of him leaking information or receiving communication. Another approach is to use a prostitute to determine whether he has revealed information, as one described: 'The only thing we do [is] we use the girls. We use the girls, we told him [her] no [now] listen, we do not trust that guy ... we are going to pay that girl 15 000 or 20 000 for doing that [getting information].'

All participants agreed that a robber will be selected for his special ability and characteristics. Their stated requirements are:

- Members should be as trustworthy as their leaders;
- They should act bravely; those who do not, are regarded as cowards; and
- The ability to drive a vehicle under difficult circumstances.

Selecting the perfect driver

They all acknowledged having been involved in both CIT robbery formats: stopping a CIT vehicle in motion before robbing it, and 'cross-pavement robbery', which has been pointed out as robbing CIT guards on foot when they deliver to or pick up money from clients, or when replenishing ATMs. Judging from their replies, difficult and dangerous situations arose in both kinds of robbery, and driving skills were of the utmost importance to execute the robbery successfully and to escape from the scene.

To identify a suitable driver who has not participated in previous CIT robberies, two interviewees said they took the candidates to a race track to test their driving skills.

Three stressed the importance of selecting the right driver:

> Who are not part of the robbing but who will be driving the car, and if we do not trust them [him] then we will delegate it to those whom we know they are best in driving.
>
> Best driver will take you home safely.
>
> We have perfect drivers. They are selected because they can drive ... because you know he knows how to drive ... because there is time you are afraid ... we have a chase on hand ... so it is depending on your driver. If this guy is a good driver you just chill.

One convict compared his driving ability with that of a well-known Formula One racing driver, saying he was selected solely for his driving ability in the CIT robbery he was in prison for. He described his driving ability as: 'I was called for the job ... I am a good driver. I was called Michael Schumacher.'

People or groups of people earmarked to handle and use firearms at the crime scene are equally not recruited or appointed haphazardly. Such people must have a reputation and history proving that they can handle a firearm. They also need to have proved themselves in the handling and firing of guns during CIT robberies.

People may learn skills, not bravery

It became quite clear from the interviews that all members of a group were expected to act bravely. Information about bravery of members was shared beyond the group, according to two robbers, because respective gangs know each other and occasionally operate together.

I concluded that robbers understood 'brave' to mean that each person should execute and stick to his allocated task, even under pressure. Those regarded as bravest have been involved in shooting with the police. Some quotations from four convicts might help to better appreciate, analyse and convey what the participants understood the concept of bravery to mean:

> But for us to choose such a person to disturb the police, that mean you must be brave enough.
>
> If you [are] not brave enough we cannot give you that duty.
>
> In such offences you need a strong presence; I will call it military guys.
>
> Militant people, people that know what they are going to do.
>
> They are so brave. Very brave ... where there is a combat.

Participants provided two simple explanations for their insistence on bravery: without brave people, no robbery would ever be successful, and people may learn skills, but bravery cannot be taught.

One explained his scepticism of some members who robbed with him, in order to illustrate what he regarded as the difference between bravery and cowardice: 'So among us there are guys who are brave and there are guys who are good in talking, but when it comes to doing, they are very coward.'

Members of the group who were not brave at the crime scene were acted against, and the other members regarded them as cowards. Such cowards would not be used in CIT robberies again, and sometimes they were killed as pointed out before.

While most participants indicated that they would buy expensive articles after a robbery, wasting money is an important consideration when selecting members for the group. One member who regarded himself as a group leader argued that squandering money on non-essential items after a robbery was one of the first issues investigators would consider. He believed that investing the robbed money in fixed property would make it less conspicuous for the police.

Splurging money draws attention

Before someone was admitted into a robbery group, the members investigated how he had spent his gains previously. The leader referred to in the previous paragraph, said people unaccustomed to large amounts of cash can on occasion be impossible to control when they do receive such sums and start throwing money around. Such a splurge draws attention. He said:

> We look at all the things what are going to happen when you got the money because some people, for instance you, never had 800 000 in your life. It is for the first time. Those are the things; we must look at them, what are you going to do. Why don't you buy a house? Some of the guys you cannot control, but we try to, in them [their] minds.

Another who regarded himself as a leader summed up all the characteristics and aims of a CIT robber:

> What am I looking for? Discrete person, very quiet person, a person who does not show off, a person who know what he is there for; and the sole purpose of that, he must understand, is just to get the cash and then move, nothing else.

A group originates when one robber possesses enough information and contacts another to discuss the information. The purpose is to determine whether the information has enough potential value and if it is worth following up and involving other robbers. As indicated earlier, it will not necessarily be a robber with whom he was involved in his previous robbery but one with whom he has robbed before and who he can trust.

The group is established over time as information about a potential target, routes and risk factors are investigated and considered. Depending on the circumstances, in the planning phase robbers will regularly join or leave the group. People with the identified skills will only join the group if other members know him.

All the participants indicated that no member would be known to only one other member. One robber mentioned that a candidate would have to be known at least to the leader. If not, several other members should know him. The reason for this is to avoid informers penetrating the group. Two robbers, one of them a leader, said that when a new member joined, his background would be checked by enquiring with his family and friends, and by putting him, his friends and his family's homes under surveillance. Enquiries would also be made with his previous CIT gang.

One of the leader robbers mentioned that they also used their police contacts to check a new CIT robber's crime history and profile. This is done to ensure that the new member will not expose the group through his well-known crime history or his police profile. It lessens the risk of identification, tracking and arrest.

The threat of spies

A valid reason should exist why a person possessing the identified skills should join the group. My conclusion was that skills alone would not afford a candidate access to the group. He should also not be under suspicion of being a police informer. A remark by one participant would seem to confirm the preoccupation with internal security and avoiding information being leaked to the police:

> You better inform me, and if you come with somebody it must be somebody that plus minus ten guys know and there must be a valid reason why you brought him here. Every time if somebody must be brought to the group there must be a reason. We do not want spies.

Most of the participants indicated that no one absent from the planning phase would be added to the group because the final planning would already have been done and new additions would cause the robbery to fail. Possible information conveyed to the police would be another reason. In fact, no member would be added after the final planning, once a sangoma has been consulted or when the group has gathered at the place where they all spend the night together before the robbery.

Further meetings are scheduled to plan for the operational part of the planning phase. Primarily the purpose is to discuss the accuracy of information on an identified target or any facts relating to the planned robbery. From the researched data, it became clear that the discussions of the first meeting were repeated at subsequent meetings. Other members of the group would test the information, the rationale being to make doubly sure that it is correct.

Having discussed how a project is conceived, I will look, in the next chapter, at how the unique demands of that project determines the number of gang members that will be involved.

HOMING IN

Tussen ons is 'n sniper, people who can drive fast, people who can steal a car. We have a locksmith among us. ~ Participant 5 (2015)

The size of CIT robbery groups varies because certain robberies need more people in order to succeed. My experience as an officer investigating CIT cases indicated that the size of a robbery group did not guarantee success. It did, in fact, improve the likelihood of an investigator solving the case or generating information. Simply, there were more robbers who may leave physical or other evidence like MO information at the scene, or from whom information could be accessed or extracted. As the saying goes, a secret is no longer a secret if more than one person knows it.

This chapter deals with the skills required for a robbery, which in turn determines the size of the robber group.

The participants indicated that the following considerations determined how many members a group should consist of:

- The nature of the robbery – whether the vehicle would be in motion or the CIT guards would be overpowered when moving between the vehicle and the collection or delivery points;
- How the CIT vehicle was to be stopped. Fewer vehicles are needed for a crash than for controlling the speed of the vehicle by boxing it in;
- The way in which the CIT guards would be disabled;
- The security measures used by the CIT company for its vehicle. This was used to ascertain what additional information was needed and how many robbers were required to conclude the robbery successfully;

- How the gang intended fleeing the scene. Participants referred to two methods, the 'start-to-finish' method and the 'start-to-stop' (some called it 'off-ramp') method. The 'start-to-finish' method is the term for driving from the crime scene directly to the safe house without swapping escape vehicles. The 'start-to-stop' approach involves abandoning the original get-away vehicle as quickly as possible. That approach requires more vehicles and drivers along with more people to transfer the money;
- The number of CIT officials to be deployed where the cash is delivered or picked up;
- The number of CIT vehicles deployed as part of a specific convoy, including both those transporting the cash and lending covert protection;
- The use of noticeable escorting vehicles accompanying the CIT trucks;
- The weaponry of the CIT officials;
- Their state of alertness;
- The design of the CIT vehicle;
- The geography of the site where the robbery is supposed to take place;
- The number of vehicles the robbers intend using;
- The number of people to be used for scouting; and
- The number of people required to 'control' the site.

Varying the size of the group is related to identifying the skills required for a specific robbery. 'To complete the team with different skills, we need driving, ex-cellphone people, ex-soldiers, ex-police and security guards,' as one robber put it.

Another said: '*Tussen ons is 'n sniper* (among us is a sniper), people who can drive fast, people who can steal a car. We have a locksmith among us.'

Participants also indicated that a group may be assembled from other familiar CIT robbery groups, because robbers and their skills are well-known among their own kind.

Two people mentioned that they experienced two groups joining together for a CIT robbery, particularly when they realised during their reconnaissance of routes, terrain and CIT vehicles that they were gathering information about the same potential target. From interviews, I learnt that those two referred to the same incident.

The research revealed relatively little difference between aspects considered for the two different types of robbery, whether the vehicle is in motion or whether it is stationary. In all, eight aspects are generally considered; the first two are different and the rest are the same:

- Design and layout of premises where the robbery is to be carried out (cross-pavement) or the area where the vehicle will be intercepted if the CIT vehicle is in motion;
- Deployment of CIT officials during money loading or off-loading (cross-pavement) or the design of the CIT vehicle where the vehicle is in motion;
- Vehicles robbers intend using in the robbery;
- Firearms;
- Legal representatives;
- Safe house;
- Sangoma; and
- Gathering the night before the robbery

'Camping': Ensuring no one strays

Assembling as a group before the robbery, known to the insiders as 'camping', is regarded as a very important aspect of the planning phase. If someone who formed part of the planning does not attend, he would cast suspicion on himself with possible serious consequences. Four participants pointed out that those who do not pitch, would be killed.

One participant said that camping ensured that no member strayed. Another made the point: 'Nobody knows where we camp. We do not want to be arrested.'

Observation of the participants during the discussion of this topic seemed to reveal some discomfort in answering the question. From the replies, I gathered that a tense atmosphere prevails because of possible suspicion and distrust among the robbers. One of them called it:

> A good question to ask. Most of us we believe ... it will cause you bad luck before the robbery, so we have to, like all of the guys, to sleep together so that we make sure that none of us ...

The get-together would be at a place identified in advance, subject to much the same requirements as for the safe house where the robbers meet after the crime, but it would be a different place. It would also, with some exceptions, not have been a sangoma's house. The venue would be known only to the leader and a few of his confidants to ensure that the information did not get out. The rest of the group would have been told by cellphone to go to a certain place from where they would be taken to the 'camping site'.

Some of the meeting places mentioned were:

- Hostels;
- Rental apartments in quiet suburbs;
- Homes of infamous criminals;
- Home of a police member attached to a uniform unit;
- Home of a SAPS Crime Intelligence member;
- A remote forest;
- A public dam (those at Middelburg, Witbank – now Emalahleni – and Polokwane were mentioned by name);
- A recreation resort in Pretoria;
- A deserted mine dump on the West Rand; and
- The house of a sangoma.

Women are taboo

An analysis of replies to semi-structured questions indicated that certain aspects were taboo at such gatherings:

- Women (even though they were used for surveillance they appeared to be unacceptable the night before the crime);
- Liquor;
- Cellphone communication;
- Interaction with anyone outside the group; and
- Leaving the premises before the group's departure.

The object of all CIT robbery is, of course, money. Planning the attack may take many months. The yield, as has been mentioned, is shared equally among group members. The skills required determine how many members will be there. That leaves the question discussed in the following chapter: How much money makes a CIT heist worth the risk?

CALCULATING THE RISK

> Take into consideration how many banks have been served - ten banks or more means 15 million. ~ Participant 1 (2015)

CIT robbers do not agree on the minimum amount which makes it worth undertaking a heist. From the research, it was also not possible to determine a cut-off amount for which a robbery will be worth the effort and risk. The matter of a minimum amount for which a robbery will be undertaken will be pursued in this chapter, as it appears to be somewhat more complex than just deciding on a specific amount.

Two participants expressed themselves in this way:

> To get one 100 000 [per robber in the team], that is why I said it is difficult. Life is too dangerous. I cannot sacrifice for 300 000 and share the cut with all the others. You see the difference now.
>
> I cannot just take a guy and force him off the road for 300 000. I can't do that ... even if I know that you are walking in the street and you are carrying your 200 000, I cannot rob you.

A veteran of several CIT robberies, who made millions from his engagements, was prepared to execute a robbery if his share was between R2,3 and R2,9 million. This he regards as good money.

Two other participants believed doing a CIT robbery for less than R2 million wouldn't be worth the effort. One of them mentioned that he had been involved in a robbery where R2 million was taken. He regarded that amount as 'cool drink' money because in his opinion it was far too little.

Some experienced robbers had stolen more than R100 million in their crime careers.

The participants mentioned several ways of knowing or calculating whether a heist was worthwhile. One participant suggested a simple calculation: 'Take into consideration how many banks have been served – ten banks or more means R15 million.' At the risk of oversimplifying a sophisticated process, ATM custodians (employed by the banks) are another source of information for the robbers on the amounts potentially available. They are the people who replenish the ATMs. They know beforehand which ATMs normally run dry, how much each one takes and at what times of the month the biggest drop-offs and collections happen.

When there is any doubt, for instance when there is no insider confirmation of the amount, two members indicated that they would look at the strain level of the vehicle's springs to determine the load. Leaf springs are normally pressed flat when carrying a heavy load.

Once the group agrees that the amount of money is worthwhile, that the risk of failure is minimal and that tracing and arrest can be avoided, other information can be considered and analysed. The first step is to analyse the available information, determine how it was acquired, determine what additional information is needed, and how the robbery should be executed.

All those present during the planning phase share in this discussion and everyone's opinion and input are debated. The information garnered by members of the group, irrespective of whether it was witnessed first-hand or not, is tested and pursued until the day of the robbery.

Vital but suspicious inside information

Information received from an insider or 'finger man' is always regarded with suspicion, even if that person had supplied information that led to a successful robbery on another occasion. Such information is checked and observed thoroughly to determine its accuracy.

The insider will be followed. If he is one of the CIT officials to be robbed, his movements during the execution of his normal duties will be observed and followed meticulously. Participants explained the thinking behind this. The first reason is to prevent the insider from being part of a plot to trap the robber group. It is also to ensure the accuracy of his information on the deployment of CIT officials and the sequence of stops for picking up or delivering cash. The third reason is to confirm the route of the CIT vehicle in addition to the day of the week and the time for delivery or collection of cash. Finally, the surveillance is to help the robbers decide on the type of CIT robbery they want to execute.

The participants pointed out two considerations when an insider is involved in the robbery. The first consideration is whether the insider is the driver of the CIT vehicle or not. From experience, I know that the driver is in full control of the security measures inside the vehicle. If he is part of the robbery, it simplifies the planning and execution for the robbers.

The second consideration is whether another official of the CIT company besides the vehicle crew is involved. The insider is often not involved in the day-to-day operational activities of CIT deliveries. This does not necessarily increase the risk involved in the CIT robbery, but it does make the planning and decision-making more complicated. In both circumstances, the robbers still have to estimate how much cash will be in the vehicle and they have to bear in mind that the behaviour of the entire crew remains unpredictable.

All the convicts preferred that, if a company official is involved, he should be the driver of the vehicle, or alternatively, the guard bearing the semi-automatic rifle, the so-called 'long gun'. The Firearms Control Act of 2000 defines 'semi-automatic' as self-loading but delivering no more than one shot every time the trigger is pulled.

After analysing the responses of nine robbers willing to talk about the recruitment of CIT officials, I reached the conclusion that CIT robbers would be more inclined towards risking a cross-pavement robbery when the driver is the informer. The reason for this is that the driver would not run the risk of injury because he would normally be sitting in the idling vehicle and it would not look suspicious if he did not participate in any of the action. The same would not apply to other CIT officials in the vehicle.

The CIT robber tasked with eliminating the guard with the semi-automatic rifle has to determine where best to position himself. The gun is not carried in a holster on his person but rather held in both hands because of its length and weight. Only one guard is equipped with such a gun, and he normally takes up position to cover the other guards carrying cash boxes.

The best days to rob

Determining the day and the date of a robbery is not done haphazardly. The deciding factors would be the day with the least risk of failure and the largest cash yield.

Six participants said that the day could be determined easily through observing the CIT company routines. Most participants were aware of certain businesses or state enterprises receiving payment on certain days, which enabled them to know when large sums of cash were being delivered or collected. Dates mentioned were the first few shopping days of a month, the 15th, 25th, 30th and 31st (unless those days fell over a weekend), the last shopping day before a long weekend or public holiday, and the first few shopping days immediately following a long weekend or a public holiday. Dates for payment to pensioners, particularly those falling outside urban areas, were also mentioned by most of the participants as potential opportunities.

One robber with a history of activity in Limpopo Province who was serving a sentence for robbery in that province said a robber had to be blind not to know that large sums of cash were transported during the Zion Christian Church gathering at Moria at Easter time. He also mentioned that the media marketing for large musical festivals drew their attention, indicating that they would investigate the possible robbery of CIT companies transporting money to and from businesses in the proximity of the festival site.

Any function drawing large numbers of police or traffic officials would also influence the selected time, day or date of a robbery. A participant who had close contact with a senior police officer and who twice participated in a robbery with him, besides having also acted as a bodyguard for a senior politician, offered a practical example. He referred to a robbery planned in the proximity of a football stadium during the 2010 The Fédération Internationale de Football Association (FIFA) World Cup in South Africa. The attempt had to be postponed because the presence of a prominent politician at the match would have increased the number of police and traffic police on duty.

It could therefore be argued with certainty that CIT robbers would concentrate on days directly preceding paydays because that is when the money for wages and salaries needed be delivered. Robbing money being picked up from businesses, on the other hand, would be planned for after a business day. I know from experience that CIT companies also do runs over weekends, but only in exceptional cases on Sundays.

Determining the right timeslot for a robbery requires a decision similar to the ideal day – when the risk of failure is at its lowest and when there is a large sum of money available. A specific time for a CIT robbery cannot be determined with certainty, given that this is influenced by factors such as the route, location and the amount to be robbed. The route may experience traffic congestion. The amount of cash may be influenced by the CIT vehicle being unable to call at certain businesses for some reason or another. Less money may be collected from a previous point than the insider's information indicated. There may be visible signs or deterrents at the scene to make the robbers reject or alter their plans. For such reasons, a robbery may be called off.

Research shows that CIT company vehicles leaving their base carrying cash for delivery are more likely to be robbed early in the day. Vehicles collecting cash from businesses for transfer to cash centres are prone to robbery later in the day. In both cases, the amount of cash will determine the decision.

One participant's explanation was particularly important because it formed the basis for findings and recommendations in the academic research: 'We know the time. [Name of security company omitted] do not change their times. They are using the same route and time for 365 days.'

Double-checking through surveillance

Once a decision is taken to carry out the robbery, surveillance is carried out. Both men and women are used during the surveillance process. No single aspect would receive greater consideration than any other. Surveillance, in general, is undertaken to ensure a successful robbery and to fully investigate all the information available to the CIT robbers at that point. Several aspects are considered in the process, and robbers also follow their own methods and techniques to verify information.

One requirement, according to all the participants, is that the routes to be used by both the CIT vehicle and the robbers need to be surveyed. That includes surveying places and identifying people to keep under surveillance on the day of the robbery in case some signs indicate that information has been leaked to the police or to the CIT company. This is done to ensure that decisions taken during the planning phase remain viable.

In two cases, surveillance was maintained at both the premises housing the CIT company investigators and the company helicopter. The SAPS Special Task Force and CIT investigating unit were also watched. The two participants mentioned that they judged from the activities taking place that the police might strike pro-actively on information that may have been leaked out. Both robberies were called off.

An alarming video released on YouTube[1], showed the SAPS Special Task Force describing in minute detail how they planned and executed proactive strikes. The video contained information that could be used to the advantage of any robbers, but I could not determine if that had happened. It did prove, though, what the two participants had to say in the interviews.

On the day of the robbery, surveillance is repeated several times, and different vehicles are used. The remarkable diligence of the route and road surveillance is evident from one participant's comment: 'Of course, you have driven through the routes for a number of times. The routes are in you, you are the routes yourself.'

The rationale for the use of different surveillance vehicles was, according to this CIT robber, to ensure that no suspicion is raised. There was also an inherent risk of limited attentiveness should only one person do the surveillance. The robbers do not slacken their surveillance routine. More than one person is engaged to ensure that no crucial warning signs are missed or that any information may have leaked out which could jeopardise the heist.

From the interviews, I was able to conclude that the actual surveillance of places related to the robbery itself was sustained up to and even during the robbery. Any suspicious activity observed would immediately be passed on to the robbers.

Having explored the various aspects taken into consideration to determine whether or not a heist is feasible and worth taking the risk in this chapter, the next chapter addresses the key tool in any CIT robbery, namely cars.

Note

1. This video has been removed from YouTube.

WHEELS
THE KEY TO A CIT HEIST

Hitvoertuie met lang neuse … to protect driver against impact.
- Participant 1 (2015)

Cars are the prime tools used during any CIT robbery. CIT robbers do not themselves steal the cars to be used in a robbery. All participants indicated that stealing vehicles was the responsibility of specialist car thieves. One said: 'They were car thieves, and they come with the cars. They never pulled a gun and point it at any bank or cash-in-transit [employee], but their job was to steal cars or hijack cars and come with the cars to us as a group.'

As with various other aspects contributing to a successful heist, groups consider several issues when it comes to the key matter of cars. Some cars are used for surveillance, others to drive to the scene of the robbery and then there are the cars used to flee the scene of the crime. This chapter maps out the considerations for the different types of cars utilised.

The car thieves never become part of the CIT robbery groups as the group members believe that would further increase the risk of their identification. Provision is made in the planning, however, for the theft of getaway vehicles at the crime scene. Participants are aware that some of the vehicles may have tracking devices installed, so they would want to ditch those as soon as possible.

Stealing getaway cars at the scene is only done once the traffic has been brought to a standstill. Those stolen will usually be the cars closest to the scene. The keys from the second and third rows will be removed and thrown away to prolong the traffic delay and congestion. Replacement vehicles will also be stolen if the vehicles in which the robbers travelled to the scene break down. In one case a vehicle was hijacked at the scene because the one scheduled for the getaway got caught up in traffic.

The participants all agreed that only stolen or hijacked vehicles are used in robberies. Such vehicles must match specific requirements and are referred to in their own vernacular.

Stolen cars are called 'hot ones', 'Dovers' or 'Schabirs'. 'Dover' refers to a (hot) black coal-stove, suggesting it is hot because it was stolen. 'Schabir' is an X5 BMW, a throwback reference to a luxury SUV that the former South African fraud and corruption convict Schabir Shaik once drove.

Other names for stolen vehicles used in robberies include 'dolphins', according to one participant because these moved quickly and nimbly, and 'anacondas', being larger and slower but more powerful car brands.

It could not be determined conclusively what price CIT robbers were prepared to pay for a stolen car, except that it varied from R3 000 to R25 000. The make and model seemed to influence the price, with older, long-nosed brands fetching higher prices. According to the explanation offered, using such vehicles for a crash lessens the risk of injury owing to the protection offered by the long engine compartment.

As indicated, although the CIT robbers themselves do not steal the cars, they are involved in the process and selection of cars. The rationale for staying away from the theft of the car is to escape identification and the possible further charge of car theft should they be arrested and found to be in possession of a stolen vehicle. From the research it appeared, however, that single members of the group would be responsible for 'ordering' the vehicles from specialist car thieves. For practical reasons, which will be discussed below, the vehicles would be stolen sometime before the robbery.

Safe places to park stolen cars

Most participants said the stolen vehicles are parked at venues where it is difficult to trace or identify them. Some of the participants explained that this ensures that vehicles remain available until the day of the robbery. It also offers a 'cooling down' period should the vehicles have been fitted with tracking devices.

Three robbers who indicated that they had stolen cars mentioned that, once they took delivery of the vehicles, members of the group who are able to trace and disconnect the tracking devices would inspect the vehicles. One who claimed to have this skill and knowledge gave an explanation worth repeating since it illustrates the sophisticated thinking and range of information robbers garner to achieve their aim:

> Most of this new cars ... they come with the original. But [in] some of them you will find like this tracker, like for instance the [trade name omitted], we know all the wiring goes on the left side. Then we go to the wiring, then there is no other option, underneath the dashboard. If I open there then I know any wire that I am going to find. In the original wiring, that wire it takes me to the box where it is and then I know where the box is.

Some of the participants gave other important answers to questions. It was mentioned that:

- Vehicles are sometimes parked in remote places to complicate tracing. Business complex and apartment block parking areas were specifically mentioned because there is so much movement of people and vehicles that such vehicles will not draw attention;
- Preference is given to parking areas with many guards and patrols. According to one participant, those people will then unwittingly look after the vehicles on behalf of the robbers while the parked cars draw no attention;
- The vehicles used in the earlier mentioned CIT robbery at OR Tambo International Airport were parked at the airport for a month. According to the robber who spoke about that robbery, the vehicles drew no attention, despite the duration, because the parking was paid for; and
- Those vehicles checked for and cleared of active tracking devices are later moved to the homes of drivers designated for the robbery. Those vehicles are parked in a roofed environment, out of sight and preferably with other vehicles. The reason given is that they will draw no attention yet be easily accessible.

Safety first for hit vehicles

Several safety considerations come to the fore when robbers select certain vehicles. Large and luxurious vehicles are equipped with airbags which ensure the safety of both the passengers and the driver during crashes. The seats can be moved relatively far back, thereby lessening the impact when such vehicles are used to cause accidents. The 7-series BMWs and Mercedes-Benz cars were preferred for their safety features. One robber called them '*hitvoertuie met lang neuse* [long-nosed hit vehicles] to protect driver against impact.'

A CIT guard turned CIT robber said he specifically looked out for such vehicles when he was responsible for transporting cash. He also referred to one-ton delivery vehicles and any vehicle bearing number plates from areas other than where they were operating. He particularly mentioned those bearing Eastern Cape plates while he was transporting cash in Limpopo.

One-ton LDVs with large engine capacity, known in robber circles as '*Indiza*', are often used to transport money from the scene of the robbery. The participants named no favourite car brands among those. Such vehicles are used for the ease of loading and unloading the money, and are popular for a quick getaway. They are also used to pick up the last robbers to leave the scene, which provides extra protection against pursuing police vehicles. Three participants explained that it was easier to shoot from an open delivery vehicle.

Panel vans and minibuses were also used in robberies. Most of the robbers interviewed pointed out that these vehicles are well-suited to transport robbers away from the scene as unobtrusively as possible to prevent identification later. Such vehicles are also used when changing transport during the getaway, known to robbers as 'off-ramp'.

Another reason offered is to ensure that most of the robbers arrive at the safe house together with the money. That lessens the risk of one robber betraying the others or stealing some of the money.

From my experience and information supplied by four robbers, large and heavy industrial as well as road construction vehicles have also been used in robberies. The express purpose was to disable the CIT vehicle immediately. By causing a crash, they ensured that the CIT vehicle could not move, thereby blocking the entire road.

The person who identified himself as the leader in the robbery used the same approach to disable the money van's accompanying vehicle. He regarded this as an impenetrable road blockade to be used very effectively on dual carriage highways.

Five robbers mentioned drawing so-called nail carpets across the road to damage a CIT vehicle. Such a steel device, for example, a pipe with protruding spikes, is placed on the road to puncture and deflate the CIT vehicle's tyres.

Having safely reached the scene of the robbery courtesy of stolen vehicles discussed in this chapter, the robbers proceed to rely on the intimidation factor to execute the robbery as swiftly as possible. Such intimidating action is the theme of the following chapter.

INTIMIDATION
A CRUCIAL CIT WEAPON

> Do you have a wife and children? Are you here to be a hero?
> ~ Participant 15 (2016)

One of the reasons offered for shooting at the scene of the robbery was to show the CIT officials immediately, as one of the robbers put it, that: 'We mean business'. For obvious reasons, the CIT robbers used firearms to intimidate the officials at the scene and to take immediate control of events.

Intimidation is a crucial element to employ when robbing the guards, and this tactical device is the theme of this chapter. Six robbers indicated that they used petrol to intimidate guards. This was done primarily to force the guards trapped inside the vehicle to open the door. A petrol container was shown to the officials. In four cases, petrol was actually poured over the vehicle – but not ignited.

In one case, as noted in Chapter 1, the petrol was ignited accidentally. The perpetrator who was serving his sentence at the time of the interview believed it to be the most efficient way of instilling fear and forcing guards to open a vehicle. He did not deem it advisable, however, to actually set the vehicle alight, because the money could also be damaged.

All the robbers agreed that control needed to be exercised over the victims and eyewitnesses at the scene, and that the use of firearms was the best way to achieve this. Most of them thought firearms drew 'respect' and believed to be the ideal way to intimidate the guards. Firearms were also used to intimidate and hence control drivers of other vehicles caught up in the traffic congestion. This prevented motorists from moving closer to the robbery point or calling the police.

Five participants cited using that as a measure to prevent personal identification and to ensure that they could continue their robbery unhindered.

One intimidated a guard by asking: 'Do you have a wife and children? Are you here to be a hero?'

Most of them reiterated the importance of controlling the scene. One of the reasons offered is that they could force the guards to lie face down, so they would not be able to study the robbers' features and later identify them. Robbers also shot at escorting vehicles or displayed firearms at close range to ensure that the guards kept their distance and, where possible, caused the traffic to congest.

The participants indicated that they would move alongside the CIT vehicle before firing at it. The shooting would be directed at the driver's side because he is in charge and must be intimidated into bringing the vehicle to a stop. He therefore needs to see the robbers and to realise that they are armed.

Provision is always made in the planning for the eventuality of the police arriving at the scene of the robbery. One explanation was: 'We knew that once we stop that car, there will be people calling the police. So, we must have people ready to disturb the police.'

Disturbing the police, one explained, meant keeping them away from the robbery by firing at them. Another goal was to cause such traffic congestion so that the police would not get to the scene.

Firearms for intimidation

The number of firearms used in a robbery differed depending on the circumstances. CIT robbers primarily use assault rifles such as AK47s, R4s and R5s, 9 mm pistols, revolvers as well as shotguns. The AK47 is the weapon of choice for all the participants because it is known for its reliability. One participant's regard for the rifle's reliability was virtually limitless, calling it the weapon that 'freed Africa'.

To illustrate the psychological effectiveness of firing an AK47, one robber's direct and literal quote was: 'People do not trust the AK47. If you shoot an AK47 over the top of their cars, they put their hands [heads] under the steering.'

The context of the statement suggested that most people were aware of the lethal punching power of an AK47. The robbers readily expressed their opinions of the Russian-designed assault rifle:

> It scares the South African Police Service because the SAPS are using R5s. Two or three in a car [police vehicle], while we will be having enough AK47s.
>
> AK47, no one asks, if. We take money if we have AK47.

> No one will follow the car if we have an AK47.
>
> We know that in a crime scene [if] we got two to three AK47 then our safety is very well.
>
> We just shoot and then those who tried to interfere, those who wanted to see, we just disturbed them because people do not trust the AK47.
>
> The reasons for using an AK47 ... people are terrified with that gun. They are special.
>
> No one wants to die when he sees the nose of the machine gun.
>
> The reason for using AK47 is that we should have enough AK47s because normal police patrol ... when you do armed robbery or cash-in-transit robbery, they cannot come close to you. They won't because of the AK47. They won't, they can't, they just run.
>
> While we are using that firearm AK47, because it is too strong, it can demolish the iron ... and they have got a long range.
>
> So the sound of AK47, let me say it, intimidates you ... we only use (them) on automatic because then they release ... five to six [bullets] at a time.
>
> The purpose of AK47 is to make this people to understand ... and to take money.

From experience as an investigating officer, I know that victims saw automatic weapons, especially the AK47, as a highly dangerous and intimidating weapon. It was an important factor when victims were confronted, and I bore that in mind when planning to ambush CIT robbers.

Within South Africa, the possession of an AK47 is only very rarely legal. It is well known that local institutions, including the safety and security services, do not use it. This means that no database for serial numbers exists, so an AK47 cannot be traced to the original owner or person nor to any incident during which it was stolen. Most of the participants know this all too well.

Robbers or groups of robbers who have to handle and use firearms at the scene are not recruited or appointed haphazardly. Such people must have a reputation and history to prove that they can handle such a weapon, and need to have proved themselves during CIT robberies using and firing weapons. One participant called it: 'That is their field or their profession; that is their livelihood. They live with AK47s much better...'

Another explained his recruiting process as:

> I recruited those whom I knew they knew what to do. Most of them were ex-soldiers. Among us was ZIPRA and ZANLA forces, Frelimo forces, *Umkhontho we Sizwe* members, police officials and those who like being trained.

Zimbabwe People's Revolutionary Army (ZIPRA) was the military wing of the Zimbabwe African People's Union (ZAPU). ZANLA was the former military wing of the Zimbabwe African National Union – Patriotic Front (ZANU PF). Frelimo refers to *Frente de Libertação de Moçambique* (Mozambique Liberation Front), and Renamo stands for *Resistência Nacional Moçcambicana* (Mozambican National Resistance). *Umkhontho we Sizwe* (Spear of the Nation or MK) refers to the disbanded military wing of the ANC.

To shoot or to kill

One participant who indicated that there were 20 members of his group during a CIT robbery, mentioned that a firearm was compulsory for every member.

From the replies given by participants, I concluded that they were probably reluctant to reveal all the reasons for shooting at the scene of a robbery. They may not have wanted to incriminate themselves in a crime like murder that carried a maximum sentence of life imprisonment. Still, all of them were involved in robberies where CIT guards were killed. Clearly, all participants interviewed had the intent to rob and shoot to overcome any possible resistance, irrespective of the consequences of firing the weapons.

Of those interviewed, two robbers admitted killing CIT guards in cold blood and two believed they acted in self-defence. Seven of those found guilty of murder explained their actions along these lines, as quoted in the introductory chapter:

> The intention was not to shoot (circumstances led to the shooting).
>
> The intention was not to shoot to kill but only to wound.
>
> The intention was not to shoot them but to deter them so that we can flee from the scene.
>
> The intention was not to shoot them but to damage their vehicles so that they could not follow.
>
> The intention was not to kill them but to intimidate them to follow our instructions.

One robber, though, told me: 'Don't give a warning – shoot.'

Another gave a more callous reply that underlined his violent behaviour:

> *Ek het na die begeleidingsvoertuig geloop waar die kontant-in-transito-beampte in was en die kontant-in-transito-beampte doodgeskiet, want ek wou "beroemd" wees.* (I walked to the escorting vehicle where the cash-in-transit official was and I shot dead the cash-in-transit official because I wanted to be "famous").

A third participant gave an equally frank answer: 'I defeat them, and the only way to defeat them was to kill them, and in most cases to shoot them because the chances to keep them under control are too slim.'

In replying to the three relevant questions, the participants used the word 'kill' 186 times.

The AK47 rifle offers more than the intimidation factor discussed in this chapter. It is also the firearm around which groups prefer to build their arsenals when they go robbing, as will emerge from the next chapter.

OUTGUNNING THE GUARDS

Ons weet dat the security company are not allowed to carry automatic rifles. We carry powerful guns. It is difficult for them to outgun us.
~ Participant 21 (Lochner, 2016)

CAS no.	LAB no.	12 gauge	38 Spl	40 S&W	46 ACP	5,56x 45 mm	9x17 mm	9x18 mm	9x19 mm	7,62x 25 mm	7,62x39 mm
						R4/R5	Short	Makarov	Parabellum	Tokarev	AK47
Kempton Park MAS 999									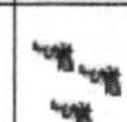		
Mondeor MAS 0000											
Soshanguwe MAS 0000											
Kempton Park MAS 1								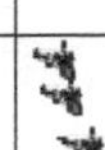	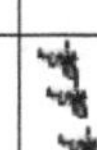		

Figure 1: Similarities in weaponry used at different robberies. Particularly important is the similarity between shotgun and handgun use.

Legend: CAS = Crime administration number

The number of firearms which CIT robbers utilise depends on several factors, including the firearms which the CIT guards carry. Responses from the convicted robbers interviewed indicated that they were well armed. Different participants simply described it as 'enough'. They indicated that 'enough' could be between three and six AK47s, comparatively more automatic weapons than those carried by the police who responded to the incident.

Adequate, meaning superior, arsenals and where the robbers acquire them is the focus of this chapter.

As one robber pointed out, being well armed was certainly no coincidence: 'We carry powerful guns. It is difficult for the police to outgun us.'

Another added:

> We make sure that we have enough firearms, which means guns like AK47. Because in our mind we know that SAP are using R5s, so we want guns that are greater than R5s, which is AK47.

One robber, referring to the weaponry carried by CIT guards, indicated that the robbers had powerful firearms and that they would always be able to 'outgun' the guards as well as the police. The central theme to emerge from comments on the CIT guards' weaponry is that CIT robbers make a point of never underestimating the number and calibre of weapons issued to CIT officials. Consequently, the robbers will always use comparatively more arms and those of a heavier calibre.

Again, the purpose of carrying more than sufficient weaponry is to overpower, intimidate and disable the guards.

The robbers also used R4 and R5 assault rifles since those weapons can also fire automatically. A summary of their weapons of choice to counter the weaponry of CIT guards corresponds with the popularity of those firearms, ranked as follows, from most popular to least popular:

- AK47;
- R5/R4;
- LM5;
- R1;
- Handgun, eg 9 mm pistol; and
- Shotgun.

Another reason why the robbers regarded the AK47 as their favourite, besides it being intimidating and dependable as noted before, is its availability.

The source of firearms

To illustrate the relative availability and ease of acquiring an AK47, one participant boasted that he could acquire one while in custody. To prove his point, he offered to acquire one for me. I declined his offer.

The participants gave the following as the best seven sources for the acquiring of automatic weapons:

- Mozambique – bought there or swapped;
- Hostels;
- Police officials who sold arms or who were specifically recruited as group members to acquire their official automatic weapons;
- CIT robbers: borrowed, rented or bought;
- Weapons used during other CIT robberies;
- Other CIT robbers not involved in a specific robbery, who borrowed, hired or bought weapons; or
- Robbers recruited from other groups who became part of the group because they had automatic weapons.

The robbers admitted that arms stolen from CIT companies during previous robberies were sometimes used in subsequent robberies. Most believed, however, that using robbed or stolen arms for other robberies heightened the risk of identification and connection with other CIT robberies.

Participants involved with cross-pavement robberies mentioned that they found it difficult to keep easily noticeable firearms like AK47s, R4s, R5s and LM5s (a semi-automatic used by security companies) hidden from view before the robbery. They devised several solutions:

- Golf bags;
- Large plastic shopping bags supplied by businesses, which the robbers referred to by the name of a well-known clothing shop;
- Coats;
- Black refuse bags;
- Shangaan bags (huge hold-alls for packing clothes and goods that migrant workers and particularly Mozambican workers – many of whom speak Xitsonga, the Shangaan language – take home for holidays; and
- Cartons packed into the bottom of a shopping trolley.

One participant mentioned that he used a rubbish bin standing outside the premises for carrying his weapon unseen.

If planning to rob during the collection or delivery of money, robbers will investigate the deployment of CIT officials. According to all the robbers, the major deterrents are the number of guards deployed at a specific time, the manner of their deployment as they collect or deliver cash and their conduct while the CIT vehicle is in motion.

My research revealed that robbers agreed that certain CIT companies as well as their employees were more difficult to rob than others. Sixteen participants mentioned one company, in particular, as being the most difficult to rob. This was ascribed to the ability of the guards, their training, conduct and their weaponry. From experience, enquiries and personal observation, I determined that not all CIT companies used semi-automatic weapons for guards deployed on premises where cash is to be collected or delivered. Also noticeable is that they were equipped with side arms. Those are smaller calibre weapons held in one hand and usually carried in a holster or on a buckle strapped to the body.

Preparedness of security guards

When they plan a robbery, robbers will evaluate the target CIT guards based on the following criteria:

- The training officials received in the handling of firearms. This is done based on the information the robbers received from informers and their own observations.
- The race of the CIT guards. The perception among participants that white people, by implication white guards, were brought up to handle firearms and would subsequently be more adept in using them. This is an assumption for which no supporting evidence was supplied.
- The readiness of the CIT guards. Of concern is how they carry their weapons, their positioning especially during the collection or delivery of cash, as well as their alertness. Most robbers said the behaviour and actions of the guard bearing the semi-automatic rifle must be observed closely. Robbers referred to him as the 'long gun' or 'marksman', while reference to the weapon as 'long gun' indicated the semi-automatic rifle. As a test, CIT robbers would endeavour during the investigative phase to walk by a guard as closely as possible to gauge his reaction. One participant mentioned that on several occasions he asked CIT guards for a match to light his cigarette. Another even indicated that he asked for directions. All robbers mentioned that the 'long gun' must always be disabled first. Notably, one robber thought that semi-automatic weapons restricted the mobility of guards. He gave a practical demonstration to support his view. He argued that someone carrying the weapon right-handed would be restricted in his ability to move towards the right because the barrel would be pointing towards his left. This would mean it would take longer to swing it to the right should he

be attacked from his right. The participant also mentioned that it should be noted on which side of his body the official wears his handgun in a holster. His rationale was that, to disarm the official, he would approach the man from the side where he wears the holster. According to his reasoning, it would again take longer to pull out and point the weapon at an attacker approaching from the side where he carried his weapon.

- The age of the CIT guards. Some participants held a very strong opinion that recently married officials with small children would not put up resistance when robbed. The reason they gave was that such people still had strong family ties and would therefore be less likely to endanger their lives.
- An indication from the guard's behaviour that he underwent military training. If such a suspicion exists, extra planning and precautions will be taken to disable him first and quickly. This is done for the sake of a successful robbery and to limit resistance.
- The physical condition of guards. Most participants suggested that excess weight or height might limit a guard's ability to react quickly.

The same arms keep popping up

Participants gave contradictory replies to the question of what happened to their firearms after a robbery. It was unclear whether arms were normally hired for a fee from other CIT robbers or merely borrowed. One indicated that he had loaned his illegal arms to other CIT gangs. It was established, however, that every robber who took a firearm to the crime scene took it back again and hid it for re-use or destruction.

During my time on duty within a covert unit investigating CIT robberies in Gauteng, I kept, with the help of the police ballistic unit, a running list of firearms connected with CIT robberies. The results, representing a continuous nine-month period in 2006, clearly showed that the same weapons were repeatedly used during different robberies. I do not suggest that the same robbers were necessarily involved, but it does underline the fact that the same weapons were repeatedly used for different crimes.

Ballistic evidence showed for instance that one weapon used at Hazyview, Mpumalanga, was also utilised at 20 other crime scenes. Those scenes represent CIT robberies in five different provinces, and on closer analysis, in six different municipal areas. Again, it could not be established whether this firearm was used by the same robbers, only that it was repeatedly used in different robberies. This represented valuable information for any investigating officer because it could be combined with other research techniques and methods. The movements of a CIT robber in possession of a firearm that could be connected to other robberies may be investigated to determine whether he was at the scene on that day. ATM withdrawals, cellphone technology or closed-circuit television (CCTV) footage from filling stations or other locations close by can also be used against the suspect, as can data from fixed speed cameras.

Most participants said leaving spent cartridge cases on the scene after shooting was inevitable. From experience I know that this is one of the most important aspects not adequately pursued for evidence by investigators. Those spent bullet cases do not only offer physical evidence; they also help to determine the group's weapons MO and serve to identify them. For example, Group A possibly committed a crime at location X and Group B may be responsible for a crime at Z.

By analysing the data, the singular composition of weaponry used at two crime scenes could be determined and a conclusion drawn that the same group may have committed both robberies. The similarities in the weaponry used for what I noted as Kempton Park MAS 999 and MAS 1 (see Figure 1) demonstrate the uniqueness. In both cases the robbers used a shotgun, two 9 mm short pistols and three 9 mm Parabellum pistols. In the latter robbery two 38 special revolvers were used, compared to just one in the former. This indicates a singular composition which may indicate that the same CIT group was involved.

From both my experience and the empirical research information gathered, the use of shotguns by CIT robbers is however rare.

A participant with a military background mentioned that he collected spent cartridge cases from a private shooting range and deliberately left them on a CIT robbery scene. Those would purposefully mislead investigators because the bullet cases cannot be linked to the scene.

Excluding arms belonging to police officials and returned to them along with payment after use in robberies, weapons are generally taken along by robbers to hide for re-use later. One participant indicated that CIT officials shot the AK47 he used during a robbery from his grasp; so he left if at the scene.

Another mentioned that used firearms, including those taken from CIT companies, were handed to the group leader. His rationale was to eliminate the possibility of being found in possession of a firearm which could be used as evidence against him.

Another robber said they kept buying new weapons, depending on the circumstances. 'Kept buying' in this case means buying stolen weapons from firearm smugglers. The reason for buying unlicensed arms is to prevent the repeated use of the same guns during different robberies. That represents a conscious effort to change the cumulative ballistic grouping of empty cases and bullets left at the scene.

One way or another, the interviews showed conclusively that CIT robbers within South Africa have no problems acquiring illegal firearms.

Apart from the importance of weaponry, robbers also believe that, before they set off, they need more than the firearms discussed in this chapter to protect them. They also take great care with their mental preparation, which is the focus of the following chapter.

SANGOMAS, WOMEN AND DRINK

> Muti for the crime scene also. That is why the SAPS who pitched, saw nothing. ~ Participant 19 (Lochner, 2016)

On interviewing the set of convicted CIT robbers, less obvious factors such as the use of sangomas, women and stimulants emerged in the run-up to robberies, which will be explored further in this chapter.

Although all participants used the services of a sangoma, not all agreed that they believed in their powers. During the interviews, I gained the impression that this was a contentious and highly sensitive matter, and I approached and handled the questions and answers accordingly.

One participant did not, by his own admission, believe sangomas had supernatural powers. He said he would rather believe in the special powers of a Zion Christian Church prophet. The reason he consulted the sangoma was that it was done in a group context and it would have caused suspicion if he had not participated. The other members strongly believed in the sangoma's supernatural powers.

A decision on the use of a specific sangoma is not taken haphazardly. At least one member must know him before a consultation takes place. The choice of the sangoma needs to be unanimous, failing which, both would be consulted if two are proposed. Two participants, one of whom identified himself as a leader, said the two sangomas would be visited and their abilities evaluated, after which a decision would be taken.

The visit to the sangoma is undertaken by the group leader and the person or people who proposed the sangoma. The following statement explains the vetting procedure well:

> Among those sangomas there are good ones and bad ones. Somebody that can tell you exactly what to do and tell you where the danger is and somebody who can say maybe where you are going with the robbery. That person must be able to say: "Guys, I see that you are going to have an armed robbery and that armed robbery will be involving a car", instead of saying that is a house robbery, yet is not that. So, once he tells us it is a house then we will see that he is not able to see what we are doing. Then we will shift to somebody else.

Interestingly, no participant mentioned that a sangoma disapproved of their planned CIT robbery. One had exceptional regard for a sangoma's supernatural ability because the sangoma once recommended that he should cancel a plan to rob a business. He followed up the reasons offered by the sangoma and found them to be valid.

There is some consensus about the time to consult a sangoma. All participants said he should be visited and consulted as early as possible. One said it had to be 'from the beginning till the end'. Making an appointment with a sangoma is done through a personal acquaintance, or by cellphone.

The last visit to the sangoma would be directly after the robbery, irrespective of whether it was successful. This visit is undertaken for several reasons, the first being to solicit the sangoma's opinion on their possible arrest and to anoint them to prevent arrest. Two said they were rendered invisible by the sangoma, which would make it impossible to trace them. Another reason was to predict the prospect of successful CIT robberies in yet unplanned projects. One robber mentioned that a sangoma was requested to bless the stolen cash, so they would not be traced through the money.

The success of the campaign has some bearing on how much cash the sangoma is given. It also emerged from the interviews that a sangoma is only to be consulted for one planned robbery and its execution at a time and not for multiple robberies or other planned crimes.

The sangoma's payment, powers and muti

One participant pointed out that the services of a sangoma were very cheap. He mentioned R50 to R100, but that is subject to increase depending on the strength of the muti (traditional medicine) he prescribes or supplies. Asked what he meant by the strength of the muti, one participant said it related to the success of the robbery.

Two participants were prepared to mention that they would pay a percentage to the sangoma on the successful completion of the robbery. They mentioned one or two per cent of the stolen money. Payment for follow-up visits to the sangoma is made in cash.

Several reasons were offered for using a sangoma's services. During the penultimate visit, finer details of the robbery are discussed, which the sangoma would approve or reject. Most participants believed a sangoma could detect whether any members in the group are not to be trusted. One called it 'to determine if one person had a bad spirit'.

A third reason offered is that he can determine if the place where the robbery will take place is a good one or whether he needs to supply muti to be sprinkled around the area where the robbery will take place. In two instances the sangoma requested that soil from the intended robbery scene be brought to him so he could determine whether they should continue with the planned robbery or not. In some cases, the sangoma will throw the bones in order to analyse which items need to be blessed (which in this context means to rub or sprinkle them with muti).

There is, however, no consensus on when the muti should be introduced to the scene. The majority view was from one day to two weeks before the robbery. The others believed it should happen as soon as the sangoma has declared the place safe, which might be months before the robbery.

It is important to reflect on the issue in its entirety. During the penultimate visit, the following items are blessed:

- The arms to be used in the robbery;
- The ammunition;
- The stolen vehicles to be used. If all the vehicles were not brought along, the sangoma would supply muti to be rubbed on them, in which case those vehicles are not blessed. One participant recalled that a sangoma provided muti '*ook (vir) die toneel. Dit is hoekom die SAPS wat opgedaag, het niks gesien het nie* (for the crime scene also. That is why the SAPS who pitched, saw nothing)';
- Other equipment to be used in the robbery;
- Cellphones; and
- The clothes to be worn on the day of the heist.

The sangoma's home or another adjacent space may sometimes be used for the robbers to stay the night before the robbery. One participant mentioned that, in case of a difficult 'job' they would spend the night with the sangoma.

The surprising role of women

Even though women are used in the CIT robbery process they are not allowed on the penultimate visit to the sangoma. I was unable to establish whether they were allowed on any visit to the sangoma with the group or group members. The reasons were not researched.

Women are used in an ancillary capacity for CIT robberies. One is to create traffic congestion. This is done by deliberately causing minor accidents which would hinder police in pursuit of the robbers. Women are also used for surveillance of a possible police presence and, when the opportunity arises, to supply false information to the SAPS at the scene.

These findings are of cardinal importance because women are not usually suspected in CIT robberies. Police and CIT company investigating officials would be well advised to focus on the involvement of women when they gather information and compile intelligence reports.

During the interviews, participants revealed that they used women more frequently during their crimes for:

- Surveillance just prior to the robbery;
- Informing the robbers of the possible presence of police or CIT officials in uniform or civilian dress in the designated robbery area. This includes reporting marked or unmarked police or security vehicles. Women may supply the information from a stationary observation point or a vehicle, just before the robbery takes place;
- Creating delays in the form of traffic congestion by using their own vehicles; and
- Misdirection. Women are introduced to the scene expressly to provide false information to the police, for example by indicating the wrong direction in which the robbers fled or supplying false information about the vehicle brands, people or suspects.

This information would indicate that women generally are more frequently involved with CIT robberies than is reflected by the numbers sentenced for this kind of crime.

An important aspect which I lost sight of during my time as an investigating officer was the use of women as surveillance 'spotters' and their reasons for doing so. The participants indicated that women would not raise suspicion when placed in surveillance positions. That is partly because women were traditionally not members of a group committing a CIT crime.

One member's view on the use of women in CIT robberies is indicative of the robbers' intelligent and thorough planning. He said: 'Then on other things we are using girls. We rob with girls. But girls can go and do other movements for us like scouting the routes for police patrols.'

Another said this about the involvement of women:

> What if there is a lady who observe for us at an advantageous point ... because there are some places where one lady who will drive - she will drive in front of all of us and she will be communicating with us until the road is clean, until we reach the point.

Most of the participants also pointed out that women are used for:

- Causing, as indicated above, minor crashes to slow down or stop traffic to allow robbers to execute their crime or flee from the scene untroubled;
- Causing crashes in parking areas to divert the attention of security officials inside buildings or security staff on the premises outside;
- Diverting the attention of deployed CIT officials by starting a conversation;
- Creating a disturbance in buildings or on the premises where cash is delivered or collected by walking in front of a CIT official or manoeuvring to limit his movement and observation;[1]
- Serving as a marker or messenger. A woman's mere presence could convey a message. For example, standing at a certain spot means it is safe to carry out the heist; and
- Serving as an active messenger where cash is delivered to or collected from a building. Besides her presence, she will also convey messages through hand gestures. One participant told of a woman who communicated with robbers via cellphone while they were following CIT officials in a shopping centre.

Alcohol and drugs are a no-no

The research revealed indulgence in alcohol or drugs did take place during social occasions. However, before or during CIT robberies neither is used. Drinking is one of the factors borne in mind during the robbery planning phase, especially in the choice of accomplices. Groups are sceptical of accomplices who abuse alcohol because it heightens the risk of information leaking out or the likelihood of a robbery failing. The chances are small of an accomplice with a drinking or drug problem being accepted by any group. Most participants believed that someone under the influence of alcohol or drugs would not be able to do his job and would endanger the lives of the group.

Another reason given for the insistence on sobriety is that the celebration would only take place after the robbery. One participant called it 'the big celebration after the loot'.

After this chapter's focus on the contributing involvement of sangomas and women, and the ban on alcohol and drugs before a heist, the next chapter places the spotlight on the fear of high technology and robbers' strategy to combat this fear.

Note

1. This intervention was portrayed in a YouTube video posted by the Intelligence Bureau SA, 2015.

HI-TECH CRIME

> Wore gloves - to avoid residue from weapons and fingerprints. DNA is a problem. ~ Participant 15 (Lochner, 2016)

CIT robbers are all too aware of the constant possibility of being identified, traced and arrested. They also fully understand the value the police attach to finding physical evidence. For this reason, they use some quite innovative methods and techniques to disrupt the investigation and to evade justice, which this chapter will probe.

As mentioned earlier, the participants said that they took specific precautions to ensure that they did not leave behind any physical evidence at the gathering the night before the robbery, such as:

- They burned and removed from the scene of the gathering every object that was handled;
- They collected and destroyed the cellphones of all present;
- They checked the data on the cellphones for any suspicious SMSes, or for phone calls made or received; and
- They used no suitcases or extra clothes.

Cellphone communication is an integral part of CIT robberies and care is therefore taken to ensure that no related evidence is left behind. Phones with altered cell or instrument numbers are given to the group members for use during a robbery. Those display only the numbers to which fast calls can be made. The numbers are only assigned for certain members of the group as well as for other key people to be used as information sources, for instance, police informers. Other contact numbers are also keyed into the contact list to mislead the police, should the robbery fail and the phone is confiscated.

Analysing the central theme in participants' replies that no physical evidence is left at the scene, convinced me that investigators need to scrutinise the CIT robbers' behaviour at the crime scene. One robber pointed out that the express reason they sometimes left cash at the scene was to draw curious people to trample the ground and so destroy evidence.

An additional and shocking example of a CIT robber's ingenuity is worth quoting:

> You go to a certain area and you do anything funny, like you shoot somebody so that the concentration [of the police] must be on that area because it will draw the police's attention away from where we are going to rob.

Other innovative methods, techniques and behaviour used to confuse the investigation came to the fore, once again illustrating the robbers' ingenuity. They may change their appearance, and even alter their speech during robberies by inserting a small object into their mouths. They may also speak a different language, use a different style of speaking or speak in code.

One participant mentioned that they use 'robber language' at the crime scene. This involves employing certain words or phrases from robber and criminal slang. The reason for this is that they do not want witnesses to understand instructions or recognise voices that could later be used as evidence against the robbers. The same participant also revealed that he disguised his voice on four occasions by placing a piece of plastic in his mouth. He cut the piece from the bottom of a two-litre cold drink bottle. He believed it changed the way he spoke.

The crucial DNA factor

Worth mentioning are the measures that robbers take to ensure that they do not leave any DNA (deoxyribonucleic acid) evidence or fingerprints in the cars they use for crashes or which they leave behind. Three participants said such vehicles are cleaned thoroughly in advance and checked for any evidence afterwards. Eleven mentioned that the police would collect DNA in the form of hair, saliva and blood left behind in the car or at the crime scene. They were also aware that DNA could be recovered from a cold drink can or any other liquid container and they would therefore not drink anything on their way to a robbery. The same precautions would be taken when leaving the scene or abandoning a vehicle. The reason they did this was to ensure they did not leave any physical evidence on the scene should a robbery go wrong.

The participants mentioned that they took the following additional precautions to ensure they left no DNA evidence behind:

- Five robbers said they wore surgical gloves to thwart attempts to trace and identify them. They indicated that they are aware that fibres from woollen or synthetic gloves left at the scene may be analysed scientifically and used to link them to the crime scene. Such evidence could be used against them if the original glove is later traced and found in their possession.
- One participant said he wore gloves to avoid getting residue from a firearm on his person.
- Some of the robbers said they wore balaclavas, which they call 'spotties', to ensure no DNA particles were left in a car or at the scene and to disguise their appearance.
- Hair and facial hair are cut or grown to prevent robbers from being identified easily.
- Stolen cellphone instruments and altered once-off SIM cards are used so that no evidence of such technology is left behind.

Research also revealed a unique grouping of weapons, which could be used to determine which unidentified group was responsible for a given robbery. For example, the repeated use of AK47s with a shotgun and a hunting rifle might point towards a particular group who regularly use that combination of weapons.

Strategic considerations

No specific CIT company, or robbery type and method could be identified as a favourite. The choice of company is determined by the information robbers have gathered through their surveillance. This means that available evidence is the determining factor rather than targeting a specific company. However, it could be ascertained that certain companies were regarded as easier targets. The reason is that since certain officials are better trained than others, they have better security measures and they apply those measures more effectively.

Once the information has been verified and a decision is taken about the type of robbery, the method is discussed. All the robbers agreed that vital factors need to be taken into consideration. Those factors determine which resources the group would require for a successful robbery and how large the group should be.

If a cross-pavement robbery is planned, robbers consider different key aspects. First, they carefully investigate the premises at which the money will be delivered or collected. The robbers will consider:

- The access route the CIT guards will use as well as the location of the business where the money will be dropped off or picked up, in the case of a shopping centre;
- The number of exits on the premises;

- How many members of the public will be on the premises during delivery or collection. Sometimes even their safety is considered;
- The number and positions of security guards used to safeguard the building or the premises, because they sometimes have good radio communication with the police;
- The arming of those security guards on the premises or in the building. If the guards have firearms, planning includes measures that will be taken to prevent robbers being shot;
- The preparedness of security guards serving the building or premises;
- Where the CIT vehicle will stop just before its guards are deployed at the target premises or building;
- The location of the police station responsible for the policing of the building or premises;
- The presence and routine of police officials patrolling the building or premises. This is done to ensure they do not disturb the robbers during the operation;
- The police reaction time. One participant explained that they would make a false call to the police station serving the intended target. The reaction time is determined in that way;
- The intended escape route for the CIT group after the robbery; and
- The number of vehicles parked in the target's parking area. More vehicles mean that there is a greater possibility that someone will notice and report the robbery beforehand. Two participants indicated that more vehicles mean that there is a greater chance that police members in civilian clothing may be on the premises or in the building.

Watching the police

Robbers singled out one crucially important aspect to consider when surveying the design or location of the target, namely the visibility of police members on patrol.

Planning a robbery includes information on the location of stationary police vehicles, those routinely present at a point, such as patrol cars on the Gauteng freeways. Three robbers said they prefer police vehicles stationary in a specific place because, as one of them put it, they know where the enemy is and can plan accordingly. This also allows them to plan better and eliminate the police surprise element. CIT robbers whose biographical information indicated that they were apprehended after 2006 – not primarily for the crime they were serving for their current prison sentence – mentioned that they were aware that static police vehicles had orders to remain within their patrolling areas. That made the robbers' planning of escape routes easier.

From field experience, I know that certain patrolling police vehicles may cross station boundaries and would react on reported crimes. CIT robbers cannot plan for that. The participants did indicate, however, that such police vehicles would not usually patrol where other SAPS vehicles are stationary.

A second aspect considered for a robbery planned at or inside a building is the tactic the CIT crew follow when stopping the vehicle and the manner of deployment of the official carrying the semi-automatic rifle. This is known as the company's standard operating procedure. Any reconnaissance vehicles possibly accompanying the CIT van are also watched and their stopping places noted.

Analysing this information makes it clear that CIT vehicles run a greater risk of being robbed when they park where they can be boxed in. Most of the participants agreed that in such cases not only the cash picked up or delivered can be robbed, but also the cash inside the boxed-in vehicle. This explanation corresponds with my experience that CIT drivers have orders to move off when threatened or when they suspect that they would be robbed.

During the planning phase, robbers will determine which sources of information they need to explore as a preventative measure to avoid arrest and identification. Robbers exchange information about previous experiences of being arrested and gather information from news reports for this purpose. The research indicates that robbers are fully aware of the practice of visible policing and that they will investigate how to get around it. Another source of information is to monitor the activity of the CIT officials responsible for internal investigation into CIT robberies.

The unique ability of CIT robbers to determine the activities which take place on SAPS premises possibly distinguishes them from other types of robbers. No primary data has ever emerged from scientific sources before this research was undertaken to suggest that robbers, CIT robbers or any other criminals display such behaviour.

Based on my research, CIT robbers also display other singular behaviours by following CIT vehicles on the day of the robbery. Irrespective of the kind of CIT robbery planned, according to all participants, the vehicle is followed in stolen or hijacked cars. Most of them indicated that the registration numbers of stolen vehicles used for tailing would not create any suspicion. The number used will correspond with the colour, make and model of the stolen vehicle. To me, this clearly indicates proper planning. One participant, who saw himself as a group leader, mentioned that number plates are removed when possession is taken of a stolen car. The robbers will then look for a vehicle that is the same model and colour and use that number to create duplicate plates.

In addition to this, the robbers will try to get hold of a registration number from an address very far away from the scene of the intended robbery. The reason offered is to lead the police astray by delaying the investigation and action, thereby creating more time for them to get away.

To prevent the number causing suspicion, the robbers will again ensure that the number has not been reported as stolen, just before following the CIT vehicle. They use their contacts in the police or traffic department to check this for them. In my view, this is an extremely important aspect for investigators of CIT robberies to be aware of, because according to the Locard and Lochner principle, there could be a retraceable lead (Lochner & Zinn, 2015:13). In practice, it means that the investigating officer can determine who enquired about the vehicle's registration number and hence a suspicious person may be identified.

Most robbers mentioned that vehicles will be changed during this reconnaissance and pursuit process. Substituted vehicles are withdrawn simultaneously. Vehicles involved in the process take up positions ahead, behind or alongside the CIT vehicle for the reconnaissance and the vehicle change is done without inviting any suspicion.

The helicopter threat

All participants are aware that the police use helicopters for crime investigation, especially once a CIT robbery has been committed. They all even know where the helicopters are parked. One participant indicated his fear of a helicopter's tracking and policing role, which stems back to an incident where a friend and fellow group member was killed following a helicopter pursuit.

A group will keep the helicopter premises under observation on the day of a robbery to see if one of the helicopters leaves. A participant indicated that one CIT company also owns at least one helicopter. The helicopter parking area will again be kept under surveillance on the day of the robbery. Any movement will immediately be reported by phone irrespective of when the helicopter departs. In my opinion, this is one of the most important aspects a CIT investigator must bear in mind.

Judging from the interviews, helicopters clearly instil fear in CIT robbers, and in the words of one of the participants:

> Once we take off, they can follow us with the helicopter. We know that the chopper can catch us. Because the minute they get the information they want - [such as] the cars that came from the scene of crime, what are they, what kind of cars - they will get you before you get to the safe house. Before an off-ramp then the helicopter will get you even if you can change the car. Yes, we can have a getaway and then we get [can] drop it and get another car. But for

> the helicopter it is easy for them because they can telescopic see the people inside, so it is good for us to have in [a] place where we can disappear.

Apart from their wariness of helicopters, robbers also find it important to keep a watch on the activities at the police station responsible for the district where the robbery is planned to take place.

Five of them mentioned that an on-duty police official recruited by the group maintained uninterrupted contact with them, whether he was in a patrol vehicle or at the police station. This was done by telephone, but two robbers said they also monitored conversations on the police radio because they could tune into those channels, as one put it: 'One of my co-accused was a police officer and he usually had a radio, and every communication they had, we knew everything.'

The police radio is monitored consistently. It is only stopped once the stolen money has been divided at the safe house and a decision is taken not to stay over at the house. One robber mentioned that they would leave the house once communication about the CIT robbery ceases. That is their indication that the coast is clear and that police action has been halted.

The interviews indicate clearly that robbers are aware that different SAPS and CIT units cooperate during investigations. This includes the proactive arrest of robbers before or during robberies as a disruptive tactic. This type of arrest is general knowledge among robbers owing to similar experiences or media coverage of such events. The information becomes part of their surveillance since all the premises where these units are stationed, are watched the day before or on the day of the robbery. Any unusual activity like unmarked vehicles (such as those bearing no SAPS markings) visiting those premises or an increase in people wearing civilian clothing is reported and regarded with suspicion.

One participant mentioned that some robbers were aware that SAPS planning took place at the premises of the SAPS officer who will be involved in proactive policing. Surveillance involves all the relevant premises, including the CIT company, police, intended robbery scene and routes, so they notice change very quickly. The express purpose of keeping those premises under surveillance was to determine if information about the CIT robbery had leaked out. One called it determining whether they had a 'spy' in their midst.

Not only SAPS and CIT company premises are kept under surveillance. The robbers' advanced surveillance capability is also used to note other changes in SAPS activities or traffic flow. To illustrate their alertness, one participant mentioned that they would return to the target area for the robbery several times to do reconnaissance. Any change noticed is immediately communicated to the other group members. This participant said: 'Maybe there is a change. We looking there are six security members and now they are four, why?' This participant explained that the reduction of CIT official numbers would be regarded with suspicion because it represented an effort to create the impression of an easier robbery opportunity.

Countering cellphone technology

While all participants said they communicated via cellphone, they were all too aware that the police target such communication for investigation and offer it as evidence in court. This happened in six of the cases affecting the participants.

To counter that, robbers use stolen handsets. As pointed out before, two leader robbers stated that stolen phones were used in the planning phase and that those were destroyed the night before the robbery to avoid leaving incriminating evidence behind. Handsets and SIM cards are destroyed by fire.

Stolen handsets are bought, according to the participants, from cellphone shops, shops specialising in second-hand cellphones, those belonging to private people or shops who repair faulty phones. Two of the robbers said SIM cards are altered by such shops to render them untraceable. In cellphone technology parlance, a SIM card is referred to as an MSISDN – Mobile Subscriber Integrated Services Digital Network. It is the card placed in a phone on which the number appears.

One robber pointed out the advantage of cheap handsets, saying cellphones that cost R100 have no GPSes. This means that they cannot be traced.

Another mentioned that a portable device blocking cellphone signals is used during robberies to render communication on or near the robbery scene impossible. He said it is carried in a backpack for convenience. While completing research I became aware of devices used in banks to block cellphone signals. It was also reported that vehicle hijackers used a portable device to block cellphone signals at crime scenes. Shortly afterwards, Nico Strydom reported on Maroela Media about a CIT robbery where a cellphone blocker was described. That description was the exact equivalent of the description given by one participant. It was used, he said, to prevent the police from being informed of the CIT robbery. Cellphone blockers do have other uses, but this aspect will not be discussed in detail here.

Answers to questions made me aware that the phone numbers of prostitutes appearing in newspapers are stored as contacts on cellphones to complicate matters for the police and lead them astray.

This chapter, which focused on many technical and technological aspects, concludes the planning of a robbery. The next chapter describes the actual attacks.

Figure 2: A cellphone blocker

HITTING THE TARGET

> They don't suspect that I am slowing down deliberately for them to come before me so that I can bump them. - Participant 11 (Lochner, 2016)

A major part of the planning for a CIT attack focuses on stopping and disabling the CIT vehicle in such a manner that the guards are unsettled and the robbers remain fit and free to get at the money. This key component of the CIT heist is the essence of this chapter.

Should the gang of robbers decide on tackling a CIT vehicle in motion, several aspects are taken into consideration. The first is the design characteristics of the CIT vehicle. One participant indicated that thorough preplanning is done, indicating that robbers think outside the normally accepted pattern. This also indicates that they carefully consider the technical aspects of the vehicle's design.

He said:

> Let's talk science - how [the] lower the vehicle [is from the ground] how [the] bigger is the possibility that you cannot ram the vehicle from the side and overturn it. In this instance, you need to hit it from the front and on the side.

A second consideration is the number of rear wheels on the vehicle. Most participants indicated that a vehicle with double rear wheels would not easily overturn when rammed from behind. One believed such vehicles should be rammed from the front just ahead of the rear wheels, which would cause the vehicle to spin and overturn. The speed should, however, not be excessive, because the robbers want to avoid personal injury.

The vehicle's engine capacity is another major consideration. The participants generally felt that a CIT vehicle with a larger, more powerful engine would transport more cash because it can carry more weight. Two of them said a larger engine meant it could travel faster, which made it easier to ram from behind and overturn it while travelling at speed or, more specifically, at the speed the robbers determined from their experience of CIT robberies. When the occupants of a CIT vehicle noticed them and realised that they were being followed, the robbers would box the vehicle in, forcing it to travel more slowly, faster or to maintain the required speed until they decide to ram it from behind. Boxing-in a vehicle entails surrounding it with the robbery vehicles to limit its ability to move in any other direction. Participants indicated that the vehicle would then be rammed from the right-hand rear side or just behind the right rear wheel to make it overturn more easily.

The fourth consideration is the size and weight of the CIT vehicle. All the robbers indicated that a particularly large and heavy-bodied vehicle would not be rammed from the front to put it out of action. They said such vehicles would push the robbers' vehicle off the road, which posed the unwanted risk of injury.

A fifth consideration is the number of gun ports in the vehicle's coachwork. These ports allow the guards to shoot at external targets from within the vehicle. Both the number and location of the ports are considered. One robber said the number of ports indicate how many guards might be travelling in the vehicle. To some extent this reduces the fear of the unknown, especially when the vehicle drives directly from its base to a client without an insider to supply the CIT gang with information.

The location of the gun ports is the sixth factor to consider. Irrespective of the kind of robbery planned, the location of the ports is always crucial because this would determine the direction from which the robbers will approach the vehicle. It implies that the robbers will always endeavour to approach it from a blind spot so that the guards inside the vehicle are unable to fire directly at them. One robber suggested that a gun port is automatically eliminated when a vehicle lies on its side, meaning that one guard is effectively removed from the firing crew. In some cases, it forms part of the strategy to topple a vehicle so that one gun port is eliminated.

To me this represents a problem for CIT companies, because the fewer the gun ports, the more the lives of the guards and the safety of the cash being transported are at risk. It could be argued that where there are not enough gun ports, the CIT vehicle could be forced to stop with minimal resistance from the guards. Other methods such as explosives or mechanical breaking equipment may then be used to force the guards to surrender. While I was concluding this research, explosives were used in a robbery, as reported in the media (Viljoen, 2015:3)

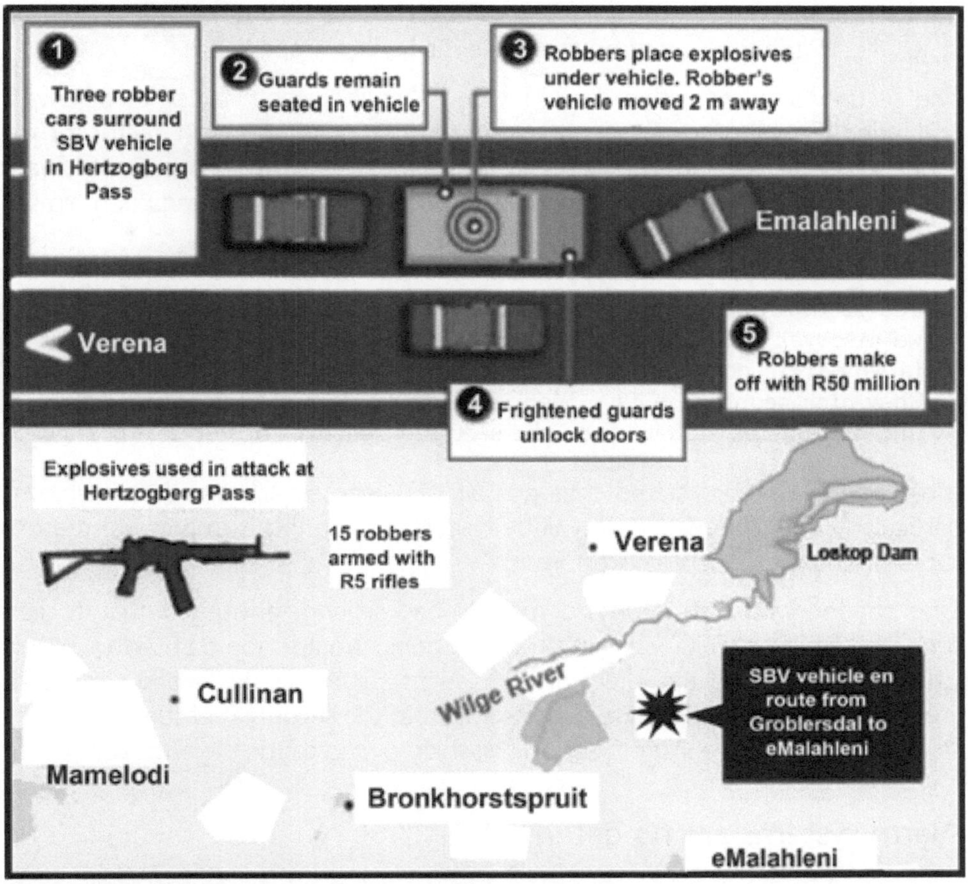

Figure 3: CIT robbery carried out with explosives

In this instance, an SBV[1] CIT vehicle was en route from Groblersdal in Limpopo to Emalahleni in Mpumalanga at 20h00 in the evening. Three robber vehicles boxed it in and forced it to a standstill in the pass at Hertzog mountain. The robbers placed explosives under the vehicle and moved their own car away from the impact of the explosion. The guards became scared and unlocked the door. Fifteen robbers, armed with R5 assault rifles, overpowered them and successfully looted R50 million.

A CIT vehicle may also be hijacked entirely by loading it onto another vehicle and driving off with it. A YouTube video[2] shows a CIT vehicle being hooked by an enormous breakdown truck.

The seventh factor to consider involves the size of the side door. In deciding who would be responsible for disarming the CIT guards, the removal of the money or breaking open the vaults, robbers are selected according to the required physique. For example, people who are small in stature are selected for the task of removing the cash because they are more agile and can move through smaller openings faster. Again, the time spent on the scene is of critical importance.

The security systems within the CIT vehicle are the eighth factor to be aware of. During the interviews, it was apparent that this is an important factor for the robbers to bear in mind. They are fully aware that security measures on CIT vans are upgraded and improved continuously. One participant who regarded himself as a professional robber remarked:

> The security features, they always change. So, if they change this, we discover this and we discover that. So we keep on learning, that is why it is not easy for professional robbers to just pick anyone. They pick people who have been involved in such things because they understand the situation or the security features of certain things.

Most of the robbers stated that not all CIT vehicles are armoured all over, particularly not underneath. As will be discussed later, this is one of the reasons for ramming the vehicle to overturn it.

One robber who had a strong military background, envisaged that rocket-propelled firearms (RPG – rocket-propelled guns) would soon be used to disable CIT vehicles. He said the effect of RPGs is instantaneous while other methods are more time-consuming. He also believes that the security measures inside the vehicle would then be instantaneously disabled owing to the high impact.

Alarm systems are no deterrent

In response to the question about the greatest deterrent influencing their choice of a target, all CIT robbers agreed that the alarm and tracking systems built into a CIT van would have no relevance during a robbery. The reason given was that, once the robbery starts, its sole purpose is to be successful. One said: 'When the car is stopped – now is the time to do our job, we don't care whatever happen. Now is our time.'

Two others said that they plan to adapt to any security measures installed in the vehicles. Such measures are updated continuously, but if the robbers are unprepared when they encounter such innovation during a robbery, they may over-react aggressively and injure the guards to force their cooperation.

A conclusion I drew from the participants' remarks is that once the target was identified, be it a CIT vehicle or guards picking up or delivering money, security measures, in general, would not have an actual influence on preventing the robbery. A robber sentenced to life imprisonment for the CIT robbery he was convicted of, expressed it this way:

> Usually when the car has been picked, the chances to leave it are too slim because all that you need is the money. Especially if somebody can say you have 20 or 80 million or 70, you start to count 15 … or at one point you see something … then the chances of us leaving the car are too slim. Then you must come with the means or the strategy. You must come with a strategy to rob that car.

Several other aspects are considered or noted during the operation:

- The positions of the escorting vehicles, if there are any, relative to the CIT vehicle carrying the money;
- The number of officials in the escorting vehicles;
- The number of guards visible inside the CIT vehicle when it stops to collect or deliver money; and
- The deployment of the guards at the premises where they deliver their service.

According to the robbers, CIT guards display specific behaviour which indicates whether they are aware of an imminent attack. My impression is that although this is not pronounced, it has a major bearing on the execution and MO during the operation. One participant indicated that the number of gun magazines a CIT guard carries on him could indicate that they have been informed of a possible attack on the day.

Robbers also noticed several other aspects of CIT official behaviour:

- Whether the travelling speed of the CIT vehicle corresponds with what the robbers noticed during the planning phase. The unusual increase or reduction of the vehicle's speed may signal heightened vigilance;
- The unnecessary switching of lanes on freeways, about which one participant displayed his observation prowess: 'If they are suspecting you can see [it] even in [on] the road. They change their speed. They press, or they start communicating with the radio.' This robber indicated that changing lanes is a technique the CIT guards use to check if they are being followed. Another participant who used to be a CIT official mentioned that he switched lanes and then watched in his rear-view mirror if other suspicious vehicles also switched. If he spotted a suspicious vehicle, he would switch lanes without using his indicators and then watch if the suspicious vehicle followed him;
- Six robbers mentioned that if the CIT driver or any of his passengers constantly looked in the rear-view mirror without having done it during the previous observation, it could be an indication that the robbers have been noticed and that the guards might be aware of the planned robbery;

- The excessive use of the two-way radio in the CIT vehicle which is evident from the frequent use of the microphone. The robbers indicated that they can see when the microphone is used; and
- The excessive opening or closing of the gun ports may be an indication of awareness.

Controlling the CIT van's speed

Five robbers, three of whom identified themselves as leaders, told me that for an attack that would take place on a freeway, they posted spotters on overhead bridges. Those spotters are stationed so they can watch both directions and monitor the traffic as well as spot a possible police presence. They are posted on bridges far from the intended robbery and communicate by cellphone.

All robbers confirmed that the same vehicles used for reconnaissance are used for the robbery. They said, however, that vehicles intended for crashes or to ram the CIT vehicle are used only on the day of the robbery.

For the execution of the robbery, it is of the utmost importance that the CIT vehicle travels at the right speed and that this speed depends on the type of vehicle.

Most participants indicated that the mobility of the CIT vehicle, as well as that of the escorting vehicle/s, would have been thrashed out during the planning phase and that it would always affect how the vehicle is stopped or robbed. The speed of a vehicle in motion is ascertained by following it. Depending on the planning of the robbery method, robbers would use techniques to reduce or increase the CIT vehicle's speed to ensure optimal stopping efficiency.

Techniques used to control the CIT vehicle include:

- Deploying slow-moving vehicles in lanes affecting the speed of the traffic behind. This forces the CIT vehicle to become caught up in the traffic and to slow down;
- Forcing the CIT vehicle to a slower or faster lane by moving a slow vehicle in front of it. One robber explained: 'You must remember they are going to pass me. They must speed a bit so that if they are going to pass me, they don't suspect that I am slowing down deliberately for them to come before [in front of] me so that I can bump them';
- Boxing-in the vehicle from the sides, front or rear; and
- Forcing the CIT driver to go faster.

The robbers force the CIT to drive faster by deliberately making the CIT driver aware of their presence. One participant pointed out that it is human nature to try and run away from danger and the driver would therefore increase his speed.

The empirical evidence shows that CIT vehicles overturn more easily when rammed at speed. Slow-moving CIT vans are more readily brought to a standstill by crashing into them without them overturning. Most robbers indicated that in such cases, they try to slow the CIT vehicle down as much as possible to avoid injury to themselves.

As ascertained from the interviews, the robbers shoot to take control of the CIT robbery. The CIT robbers themselves confirmed that shooting takes place at robbery sites for reasons of control. They have all been involved in robberies where different methods were used to stop vehicles in motion. The favourite method used on freeways is 'tap-tap' or '*klap*', where the CIT vehicle is hit from behind to make the driver lose control and for the vehicle to overturn.

Figure 4: A CIT robbery on a Gauteng freeway in 2013.

(Source: eNews Channel Africa [eNCA], 2013)

Participants who were requested to comment on the scene shown in Figure 4 and the reasons for the locality, pointed out among other things the traffic congestion. They also noted that there was no on-ramp allowing police access to the scene and that robbers were able to block off the traffic. The robbers guarding the periphery travelled in the LDV on the right. A cellphone blocker was used in the robbery.

The trend to rob vehicles preferably on or near freeway off-ramps was mentioned primarily by robbers who were recently sentenced for CIT robberies. The rationale for this is that the CIT vehicle would slow down when using the off-ramp, when stopping at traffic lights or at the yield sign after taking the off-ramp. Getting away after the scene of the robbery is also easier because the traffic flow at the off-ramp can be controlled by causing an accident or blocking of the off-ramp with vehicles.

When the CIT van is not travelling at the required speed, the first step to manipulate its speed is to manoeuvre it to the left lane. There, as described before, it can be boxed in and its speed controlled. Once the speed is acceptable, it will be rammed from the right-hand rear end to create a whiplash effect.

Two robbers mentioned that a CIT vehicle with double rear wheels on either side is best rammed from the right rear immediately in front of or behind the rear wheels, as is illustrated in the tables and pictures that follow. They explained that the driver would lose control of the front end of the CIT vehicle and the vehicle would overturn. The robbers achieve this by swerving their car into the CIT vehicle from the adjacent lane when travelling in the same direction. That is in effect a side-on crash which will disable both vehicles. Because a crash takes place, most participants mention that there is a greater risk of injury with this method than in the 'tap-tap' approach. They feel this approach exposes the robbery vehicle to serious damage. There is also a chance of their own vehicle overturning because there is a much greater impact than there would be with the 'tap-tap' method.

The different methods used to ram a CIT vehicle are best illustrated in graphics.

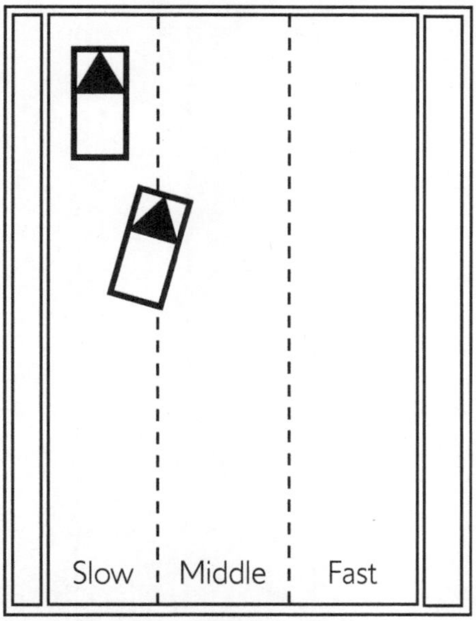

Figure 5: Tap-tap method

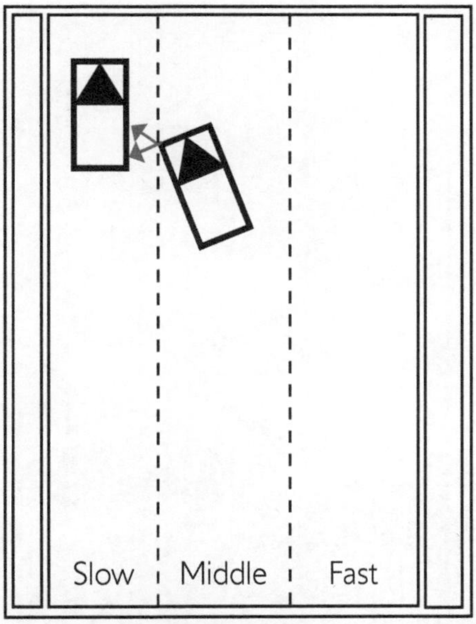

Figure 6: Right-hand side attack – between the double wheels and middle section

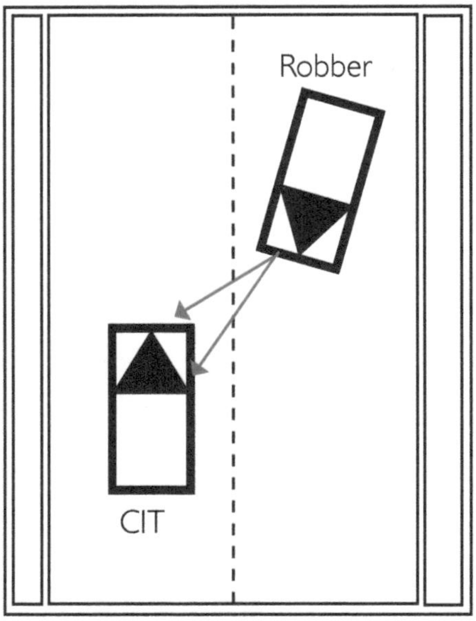

Figure 7: Head-on right-hand side attack

Figure 8: Head-on right-hand side attack (Source: ***IOL News***, 2013).

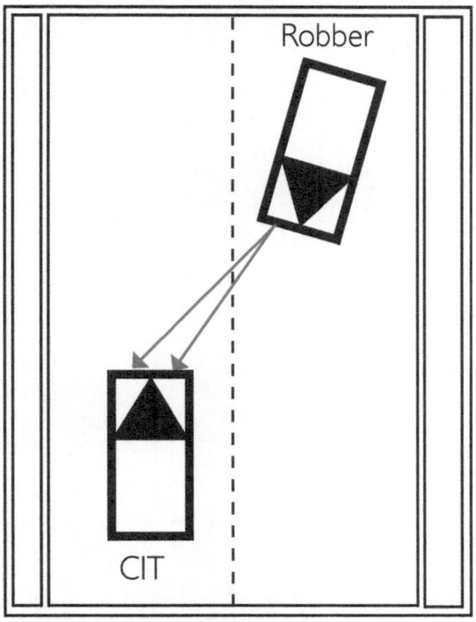

Figure 9: Head-on attack

Figure 10: Head-on attack (Source: ***Insurance Chat. Jonckie.*** 2011).

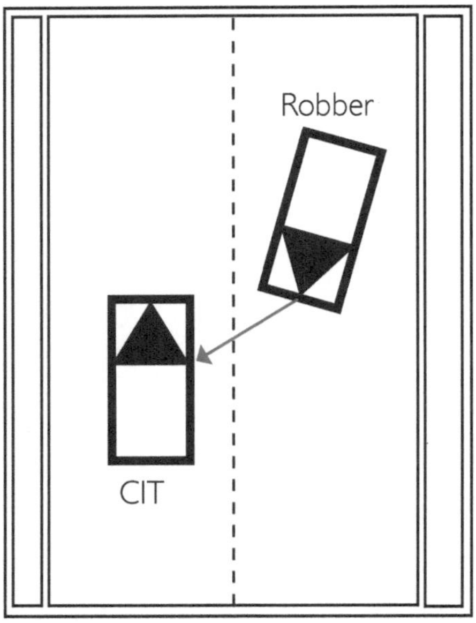

Figure 11: Head-on right-hand side attack

Figure 12: Head-on right-hand side attack (Source: ***News iAfrica. Sapa***, 2010).

Figure 13: Head-on attack at off-ramp or stop sign (Source: ***McCartney***, 2008).

It should be noted that the robbery car may not stop immediately after hitting the CIT vehicle from the side and rear, impacting on the time available to establish immediate control over the robbery scene.

Using the road as an ally

Robbers responsible for crashes said they never hit a CIT vehicle on the left side because the right-hand side of their car would make the contact. The drivers are on the right-hand side, which would jeopardise the safety of the driver as well as the other occupants of the vehicle. Besides, approaching the CIT vehicle from the left creates an opportunity for it to switch lanes, in turn making it more difficult for the robbers to control their movement.

Another reason why they want to bump the CIT vehicle on its left side is to force it to overturn and to end up on the left-hand side of the road. A robber said they want to do the 'job' on the right-hand side of the freeway because there is more room to do so. The road shoulder serves as another barrier, where it would be easier to establish control over the van or shoot it open. There is also less risk of the robbers being hit by passing traffic. In addition to this, if the job is done on the right-hand side, they would require additional 'protection' to stop and stall the traffic from the opposite side.

The vehicle used to ram the CIT truck off the road would carry one to three robbers equipped with automatic rifles since they would be the first people on the scene once the truck comes to a standstill or overturns. They would immediately take control of the situation.

Research indicates that certain methods of stopping the CIT vehicle cannot be used on freeways, but the same MO can be used to control its speed, irrespective of the type of road.

Head-on collisions are not possible on freeways owing to the layout of the road. This method is used mainly in two-way traffic where such a collision is possible. It is also used where off-ramps run into two-way roads or when CIT vehicles stop at traffic lights, stop signs or yield signs.

When the vehicle is in motion, robbers try to slow it down as much as possible. One participant mentioned that they would not crash into it from the front when the CIT vehicle's speed exceeds 60 km per hour, because that could also injure the robber driver. As indicated earlier, the robbers move their seats back as far as possible and wear safety belts to reduce the impact of the crash.

Robbers who indicated that they were involved in head-on collisions were not consistent about how many robbers would be in the car used for the collision. They also differed on the positions of the passengers. They did mention, however, that:

- Any passenger/s in the robbery vehicle would always be equipped with automatic firearms.
- The windows of the robbery vehicle would be kept open, according to one participant, to ensure an escape route from the vehicle should the doors not open for some reason.
- One of the passenger's main tasks would be to assist the driver should he battle to get out of the vehicle.
- It was the passenger's responsibility to take immediate control by using or displaying automatic weapons.
- The passenger's place, according to one participant, was the right-hand rear seat. This position reduced his chances of injury because his seat was away from the impact and he could get to the CIT vehicle more quickly.
- The driver was most often equipped with a handgun.
- The car used for a head-on crash usually carried one to four passengers.
- The participants were notably aware that leaving behind the vehicle used to cause the crash could offer additional evidence for use against them. Items

left in the robbery vehicle could also be used as evidence if those items can be traced back to the robbers. With that in mind, the robbers wash the car's interior before the robbery. They wear gloves and balaclavas, as also mentioned before, not only to conceal their identities but also to prevent leaving hair in the vehicle or on the scene. They will also not drink any liquids from containers to prevent leaving DNA.

The speed of the CIT vehicle is reported by cellphone to the driver of the robbery vehicle. Three participants indicated the reason for this is to ensure that the robbery vehicle reduces its speed to lower the impact of the crash should the CIT vehicle travel at more than 60 or 80 km per hour. The faster the CIT vehicle is travelling, the slower the robbers' vehicle would need to go in order to limit the impact.

In the interviews, the robbers also highlighted other methods of bringing CIT vehicles to a standstill. The biographical details of those who indicated that they robbed CIT vehicles on freeways suggest that they are highly experienced in CIT robberies and crime in general, and that they have shot at the police and the public during CIT robberies. Therefore, they are clearly dangerous and would not hesitate to shoot, which is one of the reasons why it is extremely difficult for the police to apprehend CIT robbers at the crime scene.

The robbers mention several other reasons for their MO:

- The traffic congestion caused by the crash prevents the police from reaching the scene.
- The robbers assigned to keep the public and police at a distance show that they have automatic weapons and, in some cases, also fire those in order to further intimidate the public.
- Off-ramps further along the freeway are intended for traffic travelling in the same direction as the blocked side of the freeway. This makes the getaway easier because the existing traffic has moved on and there is no traffic on the off-ramp owing to the congestion caused behind.
- The spectator value for drivers heading in the opposite direction also slows down the traffic.
- When SAPS or traffic police approach the scene with sirens screaming it indicates their position and the time the robbers can still spend at the scene.
- A freeway robbery allows the robbers a 360-degree view to look out for the approach of the police.
- Three robbers mentioned taking the keys of vehicles ending up closest to the crime scene and throwing them away. The rationale is to ensure that those vehicles cannot move, which would make the congestion worse.

Hijacking vehicles on the scene

All participants serving jail sentences mentioned that they sometimes hijacked vehicles at the CIT scene. Their reasons were that they needed an extra vehicle to get away because the one they used, had been disabled by the crash, or that the vehicle designated to transport the cash broke down or got caught up in the traffic congestion; or that the take exceeded expectations and extra vehicles were required.

One participant mentioned that, while they were robbing at the scene, he hijacked a SAPS mini panel wagon caught up in the congestion, loaded the money into it and got away.

I was not able to ascertain whether one of the vehicles following the moving CIT vehicle would crash into it. As indicated before, this kind of crash is also initiated from another direction. It is clear, however, that some of the pursuit vehicles are used to escape from the scene and to carry passengers, especially if a robbery vehicle gets disabled in the crash. Those participants involved with off-ramp crashes felt it was easy to get away from the scene because there was more than one escape route.

The empirical information gathered from the interviews indicated that induced crashes using vehicles parked by CIT robbers or used to block roads is not the only way to bring CIT vehicles to a stop. Two of those were chosen, according to one robber, after seeing them used in a film.

The participants indicated several methods:

- Erecting a road barrier using a stolen lorry parked across the road, with the robbers pretending to be road workers;
- Digging trenches in the road or putting stones on the road;
- Using an existing pothole to reduce the speed of the CIT vehicle;
- Driving cattle across the road to stop the CIT vehicle; and
- Drawing a spike carpet across the road. One participant said they used this device twice and took the spike carpet along after the first incident.

This chapter has shown that highly detailed planning and expertise about to how to disable a CIT vehicle successfully, is essential to CIT robbers. From here, arguably the most crucial aspect of the entire CIT operation, namely the time factor, will be discussed in the next chapter.

Notes

1. The company SBV Services (Pty) Ltd was established in the late 1980s to serve the then Standard, Barclays and Volkskas Banks.
2. See 'Cash in Transit SBV' on Redrockat, YouTube, 2012. https://www.youtube.com/watch?v=s9YZ1k6sxYw

THE CRITICAL TIME FACTOR

> You'll be caught if you stay at the scene for longer than three minutes. - Participant 3 (Lochner, 2016)

CIT robbers generally remain on the crime scene for no longer than ten minutes to avoid contact with the police and to prevent possible identification. It might even be for a shorter time, as is revealed in this chapter.

One robber said: '*As jy langer as drie minute op die toneel bly ... word jy gevang* (If you stay at the scene for longer than three minutes you'll be caught.)'

Another robber suggested that their timing was based on the *blitzkrieg* method: 'The method is being fast and *vinnig soos weerlig* (quick and swift as lightning).' These are the reasons given for using this approach:

- To steal the money in the shortest possible time;
- To avoid or limit confrontation or contact with the police; and
- To avoid arrest or identification by witnesses.

A quick – and by implication, a successful – robbery depends on efficient reconnaissance to identify certain risks and to investigate follow-up information, according to all the robbers. Their reasons for doing reconnaissance and planning were explained in Chapter 5. Several of those reasons are linked specifically to stealing the money and getting away in the shortest possible time:

- Scouting the routes used by the CIT company for collecting or delivering money allows them to determine not only the place but also the best time for an attack;
- To observe CIT vehicles from the time they leave the base where the money is kept, again with time in mind. Generally, the robbers do this observation by loitering around filling stations, spaza shops or shopping centres close to the base waiting for the vehicles to leave;
- To study the layout of routes and roads with a view to a quick getaway or to complicate pursuit; and
- To determine the location of police stations and the direction from where police reaction teams are likely to approach the intended robbery scene.

The research indicated that robbers spend substantially less time on the scene when robbing guards delivering or collecting cash. The robbers explained that they were more likely to be identified at ID parades or by personal identification because of the presence of the public or CCTV. Therefore, the quicker they operated, the fewer people are likely to observe them. They also indicated that they had little control over security staff in buildings or on the premises summoning help or monitoring the CCTV so they had to move faster than the guards. They were aware that any delay could result in the security staff having enough time to mobilise themselves and arrest the robbers.

The group's time limit is strictly adhered to, even to the extent that some cash would be left behind rather than exceed the time frame. Asked how long they stayed at the robbery scene before leaving, the response was a specific time, varying from less than a minute to no longer than ten minutes. They all agreed that this aspect is planned to the finest detail. One robber pointed out that they sometimes had to leave cash at the scene because they had exceeded their allocated time.

During a cross-pavement robbery, robbers would also try to open the CIT vehicle door, especially when the guards get in or out. This obviously requires split-second timing. In some cases, a guard will be held up with a firearm, or a robber will try to get inside while the door is still open.

Guards could also be held up on the outside to achieve some assurance that the door would be opened if another is threatened and forced back into the vehicle. Again this aims to speed up the robbery.

Using fear or force to open the door

While attacking a security van in motion generally allows the robbers a little more time, the entire operation must still be precisely planned and executed. Gaining control over guards at the scene is one of the first challenges facing the robbers once the CIT vehicle is disabled. This is the first step towards solving the potentially time-consuming challenge of getting the door open.

The research indicated that bringing a moving vehicle to a standstill by causing a crash is intended to confuse and disorientate the guards. The robbers had to, therefore, act quickly and take advantage of the immediate psychological impact of the crash. Most participants believed that CIT officials are unable to fight while lying on their backs, disorientated and confused. They also thought that any crash is traumatic. In that state the guards would, as one participant put it, cooperate more easily and open the CIT vehicle.

Either way, having forced a moving CIT vehicle to a standstill, pointing firearms at the guards and bystanders is usually the first step to gaining control. Firing the weapons is designed to further intimidate the guards. In some cases, the insider will be shot without wounding him seriously. This has the additional advantage of confirming the insider's credibility, as mentioned earlier.

To summarise, robbers gain access to the money in a variety of ways. The door needs to be opened from the inside by a CIT official. Seven robbers mentioned that the driver is usually the CIT member in charge of opening and closing the door. Two participants said he is the first person they must intimidate. By firing blindly in his direction or showing him their weapons, they try to intimidate him into opening the door. Four indicated that they always tried to recruit or corrupt the driver in their search for information and corrupt CIT officials. In response to a question about the most effective way to investigate CIT cases one participant said: 'If there is nobody shot dead at the scene the driver must be your suspect.'

Although they phrased it differently, five others held the same view: guards are persuaded to open the door by using the threat of petrol. One participant, though, regarded those who used petrol as amateurs since the cash could also be destroyed in the process. Six others believed the use of petrol created fear because no one wants to die in a fire. One participant argued very convincingly that an insider was always involved and inside the vehicle whenever he used petrol. The fear instilled reduced the extent of the violence involved and prevented evidence in the form of empty ammunition cases and bullets left behind. He also mentioned that the fear he instilled among guards resulted in their refusal to identify him at an identity parade or during the court case.

Tools used to get to the cash quickly

Robbers sometimes use angle grinders to break open the CIT vehicles. Three mentioned that they used money from previous robberies to buy such power tools. They said the blades were readily available from hardware shops, but they always tried to remove the price tags to complicate tracing and identification. According to one robber, they always tried to have more than one angle grinder at the scene because it takes time to change blades. They all mentioned that they were aware of improvements in the armour plating of CIT vehicles, but that they make provision for this with the type of power tools they carried with them. One suggested diamond-tipped blades would cut virtually any kind of metal. The use of angle grinders requires generators, but in some cases, robbers would choose petrol-driven angle grinders.

Robbers also use crowbars or so-called 'jemmies' to break open CIT vehicles, especially if overturned. One participant used a historical metaphor to make the point: 'Churchill said Italy was the soft underbelly of the Germans; do you understand what I mean?' He went on to explain that not all CIT vehicles were completely armour-plated on the underside, making this their weakest point.

Heavy hammers are used to break armour windows. Two participants believed such windows would break when struck repeatedly at the bottom end. They say it would start cracking, in which case shots from a firearm would break it.

One participant related the plan referred to earlier to push a poisonous snake through a CIT vehicle's gun port. But the plan failed, because the robber, in trying to push the snake through the hole, was himself bitten. According to the participant the man later died of the snake bite.

Two participants mentioned that they once failed in trying to blow off the door using commercial explosives. Acetylene gas is also used to cut holes in the CIT vehicle or to open the door. So too are the 'jaws of life' normally used to free trapped motorists from their vehicles after an accident. One participant mentioned that a group stole an emergency service vehicle equipped with the jaws of life expressly for that handy piece of equipment, which is used to force open the CIT vehicle's bodywork.

Two participants told me to observe for myself how many vehicles had missing or defunct porthole covers, which of course makes it easy for robbers to push a firearm through and shoot at the guards. I subsequently confirmed the validity of their observation.

Cancel rather than gamble

Timing is also an important factor in determining whether a planned robbery takes place on a particular day. CIT robbers fully realise that companies follow a set time schedule and a predetermined routine. The robbers plan accordingly. Any departure from the schedule or route that the robbers are unable to explain immediately will, according to seven of the robbers, result in the cancellation of the robbery. The reasons they gave for such cancellations are:

- The robbers feared proactive police action because two of them were caught red-handed and arrested through such action during CIT robberies.

The explanation offered by the two was that communication took place between the CIT companies and the police. The subsequent delay enabled the police to get into position and await the robbers;

- A delay might affect the volume of traffic on the escape route;
- The change in schedule might have a bearing on the circumstances on the scene where the robbery is scheduled to take place; and
- The delay might allow the police enough time to verify information and then await the arrival of the robbers.

This chapter demonstates that one of the critical factors in executing a successful robbery is speed and tactical efficiency. The focus is on establishing control of the scene of the robbery and opening the doors of the van as quickly as possible. One of the first things the robbers do after loading the money and driving away, is to check it for tracking devices. This highly dangerous phase of getting away is the theme of the next chapter.

GETTING AWAY

> After 500 to 1 000 metres you change to another car. Use another stolen one. The one you left must face the wrong direction. ~ Participant 12 (Lochner, 2016)

After a CIT robbery, the robbers get away strictly in accordance with the method determined during their planning. As this chapter will reveal, they trust their own planning.

Generally, the robbers rarely depart from the original plan throughout the entire operation. This ensures that they stick to a well-conceived plan by avoiding impulsive behaviour which could result in tracing and arrest. This relates mostly to their behaviour in the stolen vehicles they use to get to the robbery scene. In one case the vehicle broke down not far from the scene and the occupants fled on foot.

It is significant, however, that they do deviate from the plan when something unforeseen happens during the getaway which threatens the success of the heist. However, they point out that when this does happen, they communicate with one another by cellphone during the getaway, explaining the departure from the plan and the introduction of an alternative plan.

The getaway routes from the crime scene are planned meticulously during the planning phase and are surveyed well in advance of the actual robbery. Specific aspects are meticulously checked:

- Cellphone signal strength is checked. This is done by watching the handset display. However, calls are also made to ensure there is unbroken communication;
- The state of the roads is checked and whether there are road works;

- The number of traffic lights is counted. One participant believed an escape route containing traffic lights invited problems. In the case of getaway routes, the state of the traffic lights – working or not – and the distance between them are also checked. Faulty traffic lights are taken into consideration and this may even lead to the cancellation of a robbery. The reasons given were that skipping a red light creates suspicion, while some intersections have cameras. Out-of-order traffic lights also cause traffic congestion which makes a quick getaway by car virtually impossible. In two cases, participants had to flee on foot. Subsequently, they were identified and later arrested;
- Routes and roads carrying moderate traffic volumes are selected; and
- Getting off the freeway is planned. No long-distance travelling on freeways is ever considered. According to robber leaders, there are speed control cameras and traffic police on freeways, which could lead to identification and arrest.

Strategies to complicate the pursuit

Robbers also consider using off-ramps or connecting roads on freeways to their advantage by looking for opportunities to change the direction or flow of traffic. One participant mentioned that it is sometimes difficult for the pursuing police to determine the direction in which the robbers have fled, resulting in a helicopter being sent to the wrong direction. He also indicated a large possibility that vehicles of similar make and colour could use the same off-ramps or connecting roads, thereby complicating identification and possibly the continued pursuit of suspect vehicles. Connecting bridges and overhead freeways may also sometimes render the robbers difficult to spot from the air which may result in the police helicopter being unable to follow them.

One participant, who drove during a getaway, explained that connecting roads sometimes offer the robbers a choice; for instance, a three-way split. A police car following at a distance was once unable to follow them because they were out of sight when the robbers chose a particular road. Such splits also enable the robbers to change direction instantaneously. In a certain case, the pursuing police car was in the wrong lane and unable to follow them because traffic prohibited a lane switch.

Some robbers mentioned loosening the safety barriers separating the two roads the night before the robbery, which enabled them to flee in the opposite direction or take an off-ramp on the other side. One mentioned that they pretended to be road workers. They loosened the barriers without removing them, only doing that during the robbery. The reason given for doing this is that a missing or removed barrier may create suspicion or be repaired before the robbery and complicate the getaway as a result.

According to the robbers, certain principles apply to the two getaway approaches referred to earlier as 'start-to-stop' and 'start-to-finish'.

'Start-to-stop', as explained earlier, is when it was decided during the planning to stop some distance from the scene of the robbery in order to change vehicles, to distribute the money or to move the weapons or equipment to another vehicle. This appellation is also used when deciding to abandon vehicles used during the robbery. It entails stopping somewhere before reaching the safe house. In such cases, the safe house may not necessarily be in the vicinity.

Some robbers called this the 'off-ramp' method. They explained that it is usual to stop at an off-ramp to transfer the stolen money, weapons and equipment such as crowbars and angle grinders to another vehicle.

One participant summed up the car switching process as: 'After 500 to 1 000 metres you change to another car. Use another stolen one. The one you left must face the wrong direction.'

Irrespective of the chosen method of getting away from the robbery scene, it was established with certainty that the robbers would always drive on towards the safe house or the scheduled transfer spot using some of the stolen vehicles. If the plan was to leave behind the vehicle used for the transfer of the money or the equipment, then this is done. The research also indicated that no more than one stolen vehicle is left behind where the transfer takes place. Some of the stolen vehicles used in the robbery are sometimes left in other places as a false lead to the flight direction. It all depends on what was planned.

As a norm, the vehicle used to transfer the equipment and money would not be a stolen vehicle and would not have been at the crime scene. This is usually done in order to:

- Complicate the tracing and confiscation of the vehicle by the police;
- Confuse the police;
- Avoid being caught in possession of evidence; and
- Thwart or prevent arrest.

Selecting the right getaway vehicles

There will always be more than one person in the vehicle to which the money, arms and equipment are transferred. The participants' views suggest that there would be at least three occupants of the vehicle, but no maximum could be established. According to the robbers, this vehicle would travel directly to the safe house. They say it must be fast and dependable. Examples of such vehicles mentioned include:

- LDVs with powerful engines, such as a three-litre Nissan or an Isuzu;
- A minibus with a powerful engine such as a Volkswagen or Toyota. These vehicles carry around 12 people and are often used as taxis in South Africa; or
- A panel wagon, capable of carrying several passengers, with enough space for the equipment and for hiding the stolen money.

The explanation offered is that placing several robbers inside a minibus or on the back of an open delivery vehicle would not raise suspicion.

The reasons put forward for having more than one person in the vehicle carrying the cash mainly revolved around being able to put up resistance if the police pulled the vehicle off the road or followed it, or to ensure they had enough men and arms to resist arrest should they encounter a roadblock.

Whatever the reason offered, the overriding reason was to ensure that the stolen money did not disappear. The conclusion that can be drawn from this is that the robbers do not necessarily trust each other and that supervision of the cash by more than one person encourages greater trust.

Details about vehicle abandonment are carefully thought through. Participants mentioned that the vehicles are abandoned facing in the opposite direction to the getaway route. They drive to a certain point and leave the vehicle along the road. The vehicle is left, as indicated, on the opposite side of the road facing the way they came. The robbers then get into another vehicle and continue in the original direction, again to mislead the police.

One participant described how he abandoned a vehicle next to the road after seeing a patrolling police helicopter. The helicopter was not necessarily patrolling in reaction to the robbery, but the robbers were wary of being identified and wanted to prevent arrest.

One robber explained that robbery vehicles are abandoned at carefully selected locations so as to cause the police to waste additional time in tracing them. The location itself needs to be sufficiently misleading so that the police are unaware of where the vehicle switching and subsequent getaway occurs. Most participants confirmed that such locations are thoroughly investigated beforehand. The main consideration is to ensure that there are no eyewitnesses to the vehicle being abandoned.

Abandoning stolen vehicles

Apart from the abandonment of vehicles alongside roads, favourite places to leave cars used in the robbery or hijacked at the crime scene were indicated as:

- Townhouse parking areas behind high walls;
- Business or residential premises with several vehicles;
- Remote parking areas;
- Roofed or shaded parking areas, complicating tracing from a helicopter; and
- Remote bushes or well-wooded areas.

According to the robbers, vehicles hijacked at the crime scene are abandoned and never taken to any of their homes or safe houses. The reasons given for this were that such vehicles may have been fitted with tracking devices or that the owners may be able to supply comprehensive descriptions of the hijackers to the police. Either instance could increase the likelihood of tracing the vehicle or the suspects.

A robber who identified himself as a leader indicated that the chances were good that vehicles would be changed if any shooting took place at the crime scene. He believed that the police would devote more attention to crimes where firearms were used, and to cases where people were hit or killed. The vehicle switch would complicate the tracing of the perpetrators.

The substitute vehicles would have been part of the robbery but would not have been at the crime scene and subsequently not been seen by witnesses. In response to the question whether they would transfer the stolen cash to another vehicle, the robber said: 'Yes, the other vehicles we do switch. Yes, especially those we used in shooting ... because everybody has seen those cars on the scene.'

He also singled out two colours rather than makes of vehicles to be avoided for robberies: 'For the police to catch us, they are looking for blue BMW and red Mercedes-Benz. Now we try to avoid those colours.'

The two colours he referred to are two of the three primary colours. They are, along with yellow, colours that stand out in the traffic. Not only are the colours easily spotted, but the police know that they are popular among robbers, so they look out for them. This may be the reason why the participant said that robbers now avoid using cars painted in those colours during robberies.

The robbers agreed that in switching vehicles they would not use the same colour or car model as those used for the robbery and the getaway. This would draw attention since the police would already be on the lookout for similar vehicles based on descriptions supplied by eyewitnesses.

The participants agreed that they would rather abandon than set fire to vehicles hijacked at the robbery scene before they reach the safe house. They are also aware that setting fire to such a vehicle would draw unnecessary attention. One participant said that this would give the police an indication of where they should look.

However, five robbers did mention that they would set a car alight if it had carried a wounded robber from the scene. The reason for this is not to leave behind any physical evidence in the form of blood, for example.

Stolen vehicles used in the robbery are set alight, but only after some time has passed. There was no unanimity, but periods of six hours to several weeks after the robbery were mentioned. In all cases where vehicles were torched, it was done to destroy possible evidence in the car, such as fingerprints. This is backed up by the fact that no participant was arrested while in possession of such a vehicle.

To prevent leaving any clues, one robber who was wounded at the crime scene did not consult hospital doctors or nurses. His rationale was that doctors and health workers in hospitals had to report gunshot wounds to the police. He was instead treated by two doctors with home practices as he believed they were not subject to the same ethical obligations.

The research study found that robbers who used the 'start-to-finish' getaway method – going from the robbery scene directly to the safe house without stopping – did better in-depth planning than those using the 'start-to-stop' method. The reason for this conclusion is that those robbers find the quickest way to get off the roads to hide. In that case, the safe house would not be far from the robbery scene. To me, that indicates planning to locate the escape route as close as possible to the safe house, which requires superior coordination and planning.

Asked how far the safe house would normally be from the crime scene, this explanation was offered:

> In start-to-finish [getaways] the safe house must be nearer so that we can quickly hide because once we take off, they can follow us with the helicopter. We know that the chopper can catch us because the minute they get the information, they want the cars that came from the scene of crime.

Safe houses

All the robbers agreed that the safe house is an important priority about which there would be much discussion and argument during the planning phase. A safe house would only be agreed on once it is acceptable to all participating in the planning and discussion. This decision is normally only taken the night before the robbery, according to most participants. The reason offered for this is to ensure that the information is not available long enough to be relayed to the police by an informer.

The safe house can never be the place where the planning is done. The unanimous reason given for this is that the police may have the meeting place under surveillance, which would simplify matters for them should the group return after the robbery.

Asked about the considerations taken into account in the choice of a safe house, participants listed certain requirements. Such a house should be in a specific residential area or neighbourhood, depending on the planning and intended getaway plan. The factors considered mostly preclude the following areas:

- In townships or suburbs where any of the robbers own homes which they do not occupy. The reason participants gave for this is that such people are normally known to the community and the police as robbers, and that the police will usually conduct enquiries in such areas or at their properties after CIT robberies. Inhabitants of neighbourhoods are also said to speak out easily, and that they will do so when noticing suspicious vehicles;
- Premises or property registered in their names or in the names of relatives. The reason given is that certain investigators use methods to trace property belonging to robbers and/or their relatives;
- Houses or properties which are easily visible from the street. The reason for this is that many vehicles inside a property or undercover at a house would draw unnecessary attention, particularly if the property is in a township; and
- Homes or premises occupied by relatives. The reason offered is that the police know where their relatives live and would go straight there to investigate.

One participant explained that the choice of a safe house would also depend on the getaway method. He mentioned that it should be a house with a double garage or at least a carport able to accommodate several vehicles, which would make tracing them from a helicopter difficult or impossible.

The preferred location for a safe house is in the suburbs and not in townships at all. The explanation offered by the participants was that suburban people mind their own business behind high boundary walls and that there is very little visitor or vehicle traffic; so, the robbers would easily notice police vehicles approaching. They also said that suburban people would already be at work by the time the robbers arrived at the safe house, which means that there are fewer possible eyewitnesses. This leads to the conclusion that many township people are at home during the daytime, and that 'natural' observation would be more likely on such properties as they do not generally have high walls. Townhouses or garden cottages were singled out as more suitable safe houses.

Owners of safe houses are required to be fully trustworthy. In most cases, they would have been investigated beforehand to check for any links with the police. Owners are compensated both before the robbery and afterwards. The reason for this is to ensure that the owners depend on the robbers for the full payment and would therefore not be tempted to give away information before the robbery. The amounts the participants said were paid to safe house owners varied from R50 000 to R300 000, depending on the take.

Where properties were rented, the participants immediately started building a cover. One robber mentioned that he introduced himself to the neighbours as a long-term insurance salesperson. He placed brochures from well-known insurance companies on his car's dashboard to mislead the neighbours. The rented properties were in Sandton, Bryanston and Fourways in the greater Johannesburg area, and at Garsfontein, Waterkloof, Murrayfield and Equestria in Pretoria. Most participants notably described such neighbourhoods as affluent.

The interviewees generally suggested that once they reached the safe house, the robbers would spend quite some time there to relax and divide the cash. The explanation given for this, as one robber said, is that the police 'are all over around'. Others suggested that more time was spent in the safe house after a robbery in rural areas, explaining:

> Outside place like North West ... those places ... when there is a robbery, they will close all the areas most of the time. They close the direction to Johannesburg. Then we know we must not go out. Then we will stay probably from 10 o' clock in the morning to half-past nine [at night], then we communicate with the phone.

My observation as an investigator, along with the information supplied during in-depth interviews, is that once they have reached the safe house, robbers relax their vigilance about not leaving DNA evidence, despite all the earlier precautions described in this chapter. Once inside the house, it is time to divide the stolen money and to decide what happens to those huge sums, which is discussed in the following chapter.

LOTS AND LOTS OF MONEY

> Expensive cars ... overseas trips ... entertain women ... buy clothes ... bought a townhouse in distinguished suburb. ~ Participant 5 (Lochner, 2016)

In several respects, CIT robbers display ideal teamwork. Conceiving the idea, assembling a group, producing a leader and fine-tuning the attack, as discussed in previous chapters, all show selflessness. But once they have the money, a decidedly human frailty surfaces. The money, that proverbial root of all evil, might jeopardise the entire operation, as this chapter illustrates.

Robbers say quite frankly that the stolen money is always divided under a cloud of distrust. The notion that the money is not divided equally, is also singled out as the main reason why disenchanted accomplices supply information to the police about a robbery. This lingering suspicion about the equal distribution of the money remains despite the prior discussion and planning in the finest detail.

Such suspicion is recognised and overcome by introducing appropriate measures. As mentioned before, at least two or preferably more robbers will be placed in charge of guarding the cash all the time until it is divided in the presence of most of the group at the safe house.

This is by no means the end of the problems caused by the stolen money. The robbers agree that it would always cause problems if any suspect is caught by the police in possession of a large amount of cash.

It is significant that no family members are involved when the robbery is committed. Some of the robbers will also avoid any direct contact with each other after leaving the safe house with their share of the money.

Hiding the stolen money

Following a robbery in Port Elizabeth, one robber did not want to be found with the money in his possession. He bought a box of wine, substituted some of the bottles with cash and couriered the container to himself at his Johannesburg address.

Most participants divided the money into smaller amounts and hid it, so as to not lose it all should they get arrested, or should the police find one hiding place. Explaining the possession of smaller amounts is easier than accounting for large amounts. Smaller amounts also do not draw as much attention. Moreover, the participants believed that the police would not be as ready to investigate the source and possession of smaller amounts.

The robbers found ingenious places to hide the money. Some hid it in:

- An outside or pit toilet;
- Cultivated or uncultivated soil in a former homeland;
- A home or inside apartment ceilings;
- A storage unit like a storeroom or garage, which can be rented monthly. One participant suggested he would pay R500 per month for a year to store R4 000 000 in cash;
- Shoe holders hidden in children's rooms;
- An attorney's offices;
- An office safe. The participant used to be a policeman. He reckons he would have supplied the alibi that he had confiscated the large amount of cash doing his work as a policeman; and
- Outbuildings on their home premises. Reference was made to storerooms and garages. One robber indicated that he hid money in his swimming pool pump which was installed in an outbuilding.

All participants were aware that financial institutions are obliged to report large cash deposits to the relevant authorities. Therefore they had to find various ways to launder the money. One participant regularly deposited small amounts into his mother's personal account without her knowledge. Another deposited cash into the account of a family-owned second-hand car business which was later paid back to him. A third participant said that he used one fake ID to open three accounts in family names and deposited and withdrew money at will.

Buying expensive cars

The second-hand car business was singled out as an ideal way to avoid 'unnecessary' questions when expensive cars are bought for cash. The strategy to avoid such questions is to ask older family members to do the buying or the making of payments. If questions are asked about the money, the reply would be that it is pension money. Vehicles were bought in various ways, of which buying from second-hand dealers or through family members who own businesses were most common.

One participant's explanation proves the ease of buying many vehicles without raising suspicion:

> When I was arrested, I was driving a BMW 525 and I had a Nissan double cab 4x4 ... in my life I bought about 26 cars - without anybody asking questions.

All participants but one bought luxury and therefore expensive vehicles with the stolen money. Brands such as BMW, Mercedes-Benz, four-wheel drives of various brands while Volkswagen Golf and different types of sports cars were mentioned. One said that he always dreamt of owning a particular sports Golf with a specialised gearbox, and he bought one through a used-car dealer. One participant was so obsessed with a vehicle of a specific brand and model that he spent the bulk of his loot on it. Another, referring to the association of luxury with riches, said: 'A car speaks for itself.'

Apart from buying vehicles to hide or get rid of stolen money, the research information also points to other ways of covering up the cash.

Buying property

All the robbers had both fixed properties registered in their names and moving assets when they committed the crimes for which they were serving prison sentences. In none of the cases did the police attach such assets during the trial as proof of proceeds from crime. Moving assets, like the cars used in the crime, were however attached. The fixed assets in the robbers' possession when committing the crimes they were sentenced for, included:

- Apartments;
- Townhouses;
- Houses; and
- A smallholding.

While they were awaiting trial, two robbers bought fixed property. Replying to the question of how he spent his money one robber said:

> What I can tell you is that, my age of people, I bought property even though I am in prison. If I go outside, I will not sleep in the bush. I will sleep in my property.

Fixed property is also used to mislead police tracing efforts. One said:

> I have a townhouse where I hide, where sometimes my wife will come and visit with the children. I had my own house, but there are [other] townhouses that I bought.

Another mentioned that he used a property that he bought to hide his family to complicate tracing and arrest.

One participant was critical of his co-robbers buying property for other people. He said:

> Robbers spend their money not wisely. There are so many. Sometimes it is difficult because when we get money, we take its own, each and everyone takes its own way. I hate that there are guys that bought houses for girlfriends, townhouses for girlfriends and cars for girlfriends. I cannot do that. I don't want to have a problem in the near future. Because once I buy a house to that girlfriend then it means I have to keep on following her. So, I can give her something, but I cannot buy her a house.

One participant said he took his family to Cape Town for a holiday where they stayed at his apartment. He also gave some of the stolen money to his father, who used it to buy a farm.

A robber who presented himself as a spendthrift said he bought an apartment and fitted it luxuriously with expensive furniture and electronic gadgets.

Another robber stated his spending priorities as firstly, building a house, then paying his children's school fees, and finally, buying an expensive vehicle.

Splashing out on holidays, luxuries and women

One participant summarised his indulgences: 'Expensive cars ... overseas trips ... entertain women ... buy clothes ... bought a townhouse in [a] distinguished suburb.'

Luxury hotels and holiday resorts were popular. Destinations included Cape Town, Durban, the Victoria Falls and Mozambique. One participant mentioned several trips into other parts of Africa for which stolen money was used.

While some older participants made no direct reference to prostitutes, they did indicate that they used some of the money to spoil wives and girlfriends. Most admitted that they have spent time with prostitutes, one mentioning that they paid between R15 000 and R20 000 per visit. One mentioned a professional prostitute who advertised her services in the media. Significantly, four participants said they paid for prostitutes' services for two weeks and spent 24 hours in their company. They normally travelled on such occasions. This was done to avoid tracing and normally took place immediately after a robbery.

The robbers also visited exclusive nightclubs in Johannesburg, Pretoria, Pietermaritzburg, Durban and Bloemfontein. Most boasted that they went to the fanciest and most expensive restaurants in their most extravagant cars and outfits. The sole reason was to draw the attention of women. Money was used expansively and so ostentatiously that everyone around would notice.

Casinos were visited with the sole purposes of getting stolen money into circulation and building a reputation of being regular casino visitors. Being a casino regular offered an alibi when cash was found in their possession.

The robbers also used the money to buy:

- A comfortable lifestyle offering only the best of everything;
- Expensive furniture and domestic electronic appliances;
- Expensive car radios and accessories;
- Exceptionally expensive groceries;
- Expensive clothes, especially those bought from designer boutiques, handbags; and
- Expensive shoes bought from Dunhill, Levi's, Bon Ami, Gerani and Damiani.

One participant said he did not spend his money on prostitutes, instead, he associated with women who owned luxury apartments and houses, as well as women in occupations such as medical doctors, accountants and academics. He also spent money on treating female attorneys, buying them expensive jewellery and taking them to social functions.

Social life after a robbery

The robbers led active social lives after the crime, albeit mostly in their own circles. The post-robbery social activities and interactions of CIT robbers who participated in this research fall into two broad categories. Six of them only had contact with the others when planning the next crime or when there was an inkling of suspicion that a member of the group had spilt information, especially to the police, and when a decision needed to be made on action against such a person.

The 12 members who got together after the robberies did so only to:

- Celebrate success;
- Pay homage to the deceased should someone have been killed;
- Seek female company;

- Spoil themselves with expensive food and drink;
- Splash money; and
- Boast of excessive cash, expensive clothes and jewellery.

Some robbers chose social isolation as a way of limiting access to information about themselves to only a select few trustworthy people. Particularly some older people mentioned that they did not want to socialise with others. Some moved away from their homes, in certain cases to live permanently elsewhere.

Two participants in the 31 to 35 age group socialised separately with private people during semi-formal functions and subsequently started love affairs. The first function was an art exhibition at a well-known Gauteng university, where the man befriended a university professor. He later started a second love affair. It started in an exclusive restaurant, where he met a senior lecturer from another Gauteng university. In the third case, the occasion was the launch of a new product from a well-known insurance company, where the robber befriended someone in the legal profession.

Both participants said the women were unaware of their criminal activities but later suspected that they may have been involved in something underhand. Both said the suspicion arose because the income from the careers they purported to have, did not match their spending habits. The participants said they both hid some of the stolen money in their partners' homes without their knowledge. One participant mentioned that when one woman became aware of his criminal activities, she blackmailed him by threatening to expose his identity and activities. Their relationship ceased when he contributed financially towards buying an asset for her.

I followed up on the particulars about the two university members supplied by the participant and found them to be true. The names of the people and the institutions are not mentioned here for ethical reasons. The information about the legal person was not followed up, and the person's name is also withheld for ethical reasons.

Stolen money was not only used to buy assets, luxuries and to impress potential lady friends as described in this chapter. As the next chapter will point out, it served also to snare police members as part of a larger strategy of outwitting the law.

COPS OR ROBBERS?

There is always a way of keeping contact with a policeman. Corrupt them little by little. ~ Participant 16 (Lochner, 2016)

Whatever perceptions I may have had beforehand about why the police make insufficient progress in prosecuting CIT robberies were cast in a different light as a result of this research. The first is that, once again, the robbers seem to know much more about the police than the police know about them. The second is that a rogue police element involved in CIT robberies sometimes surprised even the robbers. These issues are addressed in this chapter.

Surveillance, as repeatedly mentioned before, plays an extremely important role in CIT robbers' planning. The way in which they check information and the actions of others repeatedly illustrate the thoroughness of the planning. The robbers do not limit their observation of police members to their physical appearance but they will also note the vehicles they use to prevent and investigate crime. CIT robbers have methods and sources of their own to access information to ensure the successful execution of their robberies. It is crucial for them to check and investigate such sources, especially those which they can observe themselves. The layman might regard this as unimportant, but this research proves that CIT robbers generate valuable information. This even includes information about helicopters deployed by the police and CIT companies, and about the activities taking place within police and company premises respectively.

During surveillance, the robbers look for any visible or attempted invisible – covert, in police terms – signs of police presence in areas where CIT robberies are planned. This includes not only the immediate vicinity of the designated robbery site, but also the routes and roads to and from the chosen location. Visible signs include police vehicles, police officials patrolling on foot as well as those standing and monitoring the roads.

Any increase or decrease in police numbers will raise the robbers' suspicions. Slow-moving traffic on roads will do the same, since according to one robber:

> You see, like, on the freeway every [most] cars are moving fast, but on that day, you find that there is a car that are [is] moving slowly. Look at that car, those guys they look like cops. It is easy to see the police even if they can change their clothes [appearance].

From the ease with which the robbers recognise police officials who are trying to act covertly, I can only conclude that the robbers have well-honed observation skills. Two participants said they looked at number plates. They claimed those used on police cars were metal and not plastic, although I could not confirm or reject the claim from my own observation. It was also pointed out that the number plates must fit the vehicle model: a new car with old Gauteng numbers looked suspicious.

Recognising the police 'look'

Two robbers mentioned looking at the physique, clothing and hairstyles of people at the designated robbery site as well as the proposed routes. They claimed investigating officers are generally overweight, and those in civilian clothing do not wear T-shirts. Because of their training, their shirts are always tucked in. The traditional police members who investigate ordinary crime, as well as those who investigate CIT robberies, wear, according to the participants, their hair close-cropped, with the majority shaving their heads altogether. The robbers called the style 'cheese head'.

The two participants arrested as a result of proactive police action said that a special police unit which usually operates in uniform formed part of that action. They claimed that it was general knowledge among robbers. Subsequently, they were always on the look-out for white people with military haircuts in vehicles.

They say the racial profile of the occupants of cars often appeared particularly suspicious. Based on perceptions created during the previous political dispensation, some robbers believed that two people from different racial groups seldom travel together – unless they are police officers.

One participant's views are worth repeating. They comprise the robbers' general view and have significant relevance for investigations into CIT robberies, again with specifics about police units removed for ethical reasons:

> Because we are also very good to identify the trap it is very easy ... on this road, we know exactly what type of people do we find or what type of vehicles are always passing here. And then today I see here is a car, it is just stationed on the other side of the road. [In] that car there is a white man and an Indian, another car is a white man

> and a black man, and [in] another car maybe it is a black man and an Indian. Then automatically it raises a suspicion and [that] these guys are special detectives.
>
> You know most of them are big, especially the detectives.
>
> The other advantage that we always have is we normally know them. I know that this guy is working for [name omitted] and this guy is working for [name omitted], and he is the one that arrested me.
>
> This guy in [name omitted] and their cars ... we are able to know the cars from the police station.
>
> We are able to send our people to check the cars in a certain department of police station and detectives, and then we know that number so and so Toyota with this colour belongs to certain police station, especially during that period that we want to hit.
>
> If they bring something or somebody from the Free State or Durban then again we'll ask ourselves why the Durban people are around this area, what are they looking for. So, this is a maybe a trap. Let us check this out and see next week.

Cops on the robbers' side

One may assume that the police and robbers operate on opposing sides. This may not necessarily be the case with every robbery. Two participants in the interviews spoke of police officials they recruited to be part of a CIT robbery who did observations with them and compiled information.

One robbery was called off because a police officer was part of another group which followed the same vehicle that they were scouting. A robber said:

> While we were scouting the vehicle, we realised that another group was also scouting the same vehicle and we suspected that the finger-man was providing information to other robbers. We recognise [name omitted], who is a police official, and we later approached him and because we suspected the finger-man to be an informant, we did call off the robbery.

Generally, the robbers would rather call off a robbery than risk confrontation and arrest. One robber said: '*Moet nooit op polisie skiet – as iets verdag is – stop die roof.* We give sign – *vuis* – has to stop. Open *vuis* – *beteken ons stop en split.* (Don't ever shoot at the police. If something is suspicious, stop the robbery. We give a sign – a fist – it must stop. Open fist means we stop and split.)'

The robbers made many references to police involvement in CIT robberies. One said in response to a question of how many police officials were involved: 'A lot. Nearly, let me say out of ten, five or six they are involved.'

Another participant told of two police officers who were recruited as members of a robbery gang. Their role was shooting. It turned out that they had encountered each other before, because as the participant put it, '*Een was van Security Branch en ander MK. Die twee ken mekaar omdat SAP die MK gearresteer het. Die MK was in Oos-Duitsland drie jaar.* (One was from the Police Security Branch and the other *Umkhontho we Sizwe*. They knew each other because the SAP arrested the MK. The MK was in East Germany for three years.)'

In four cases where one participant was involved, the safe houses belonged to a corrupt police officer. While he and his fellow group members hid in those houses, the premises were visited by police members who were involved in the four cases in some way or another. The purpose of the visits was to collect bribes.

One participant told cynically of the ongoing process of recruiting police members. He said there is always a way of keeping contact with a police officer. Robbers always have money and they can buy drinks in the middle of the month. They also have nice houses. With their luxuries, they corrupt police officer 'little by little' until, as he put it, 'that time you sell the R5.'

'Cops and robbers,' according to one participant, 'like same places and same women, but differ in language.'

Recruiting members of the police, as described in this chapter, is only part of robber groups' strategy to outwit the law. How they recruit insiders from other branches of the legal system and how the robbers use them is discussed in the next chapter.

DEFEATING THE ENDS OF JUSTICE

> Crime money - the only people who benefit from it is lawyers. ~ Participant 15 (Lochner, 2016)

In their replies, the participants' responses revealed the extent to which officials in the criminal justice system are bribed, and this is striking. The chapter focuses on who gets bribed and for which purposes.

The credibility of the robbers' versions should not be rejected out of hand. As a former police official, I knew and am still aware of current and former police members and units who were and are responsible for CIT investigations. Some of the information revealed by the participants they could only have been aware of if they had personal experience and contact with officials or units.

Conversely, the participants had respect for honourable officials. One participant, for example, expressed high regard for the prosecutor who handled his case. He mentioned that some of her colleagues betrayed her in the court process by revealing confidential information to him and removing evidence from the store. Two participants also expressed high regard for the police officials who arrested them, and one thought a police officer was very clever.

Bribing police officials

In Chapter 17, participants mentioned how important police involvement was in carrying out a successful robbery. Collectively, the participants said police officials were bribed in order to:

- Be close to the robbery scene to convey to the robbers by cellphone information broadcast over the police radio;
- Be in the specific area where the robbery is planned to render 'protection';
- Supply police firearms for use during robberies;
- Destroy exhibits;
- Supply information on the investigation and to inform the robbers if they have been identified as suspects;
- Supply information about the time of their arrest so they can arrange a legal representative or flee;
- Ensure bail is facilitated by not opposing it;
- Supply information on where the investigator filed exhibits for safekeeping so it can be stolen and destroyed;
- Supply the daily whereabouts of the investigator or the investigating teams;
- Eliminate or intimidate witnesses;
- Steal or destroy case dockets implicating robbers;
- Help or facilitate escape;
- Remove or destroy certain parts of case dockets (mostly self-incriminating evidence such as confessions or admissions of guilt);
- Not carry out the arrest of robbers;
- Delay arrests, even after the perpetrator is identified; or
- Release robbers after their court appearance but before the trial starts. The fact that police officials are regularly bribed, was confirmed by one participant saying simply: 'Yes, it happened several times.' Another mentioned that he bribed several police officers. In the case for which he was serving a prison sentence, he said, he bribed a police officer with R600 000 to destroy evidence. It was paid in four instalments. A third participant was unsure of the amount he had spent on bribing police officers. He mentioned a million rand.

The extent and ease with which officials in the criminal justice system are bribed emerged clearly from the following description given by a participant:

> Like I got a case. Then you (using me as an example) are the one who is handling my case. After some time, you arrest me. Then I talk to you and say yes, [name omitted to prevent identification] where is the money? I say don't arrest me. I can give you 20 now. Then I give him 20 [R20 000]. Then we start to chat ... I am looking for this one. I got his case. That is my friend. Then I tell that guy that you are looking for him and you are a good guy - you can take something to him then he gives you something and then your relationship starts to bond.

Another participant described how easily police officials are bribed to ensure that CIT robbers are set free:

> Apparently the first one he took our money. Apparently, we organised - I had a wife and the other girlfriends - he said that we would give him R20 000, 2 000 each he will open a bail for us, on the first one charge. So, all collected that money and gave it to him and he just determined bail. On the second charge we wanted to bribe - apparently it was never successful. He was fearful that he would get arrested because, you see, among us, one of us was a police officer. So, he was afraid that if you take a bribe, this guy is a police officer, something would backfire and you [he] may lose your job.

Bribed police officers include:

- Officials on routine patrol who by chance wanted to remand or arrest the participant for a minor infringement. The participant was worried that the officials would connect him to a robbery;
- Policemen working at courts;
- Policemen on duty at police stations;
- The investigating officer;
- In certain cases, officials who were part of an investigating team;
- Officials who compiled covert information on CIT cases; and
- Officials attached to crime intelligence gathering units.

In most police bribery cases the original act was initiated by the robbers themselves. It was only in one case in which a family member initiated the bribe. Conversely, contact with a view to bribery was also started by police members investigating CIT cases. It is suggested that such corrupt police officers know where and when the robbers were arrested and held. They would then approach the CIT robbers in custody. One participant said: 'I was approached by [name withheld]. He ask money from me to let me go.'

Bribing magistrates and prosecutors

Contact with prosecutors or magistrates with the intention of bribery was initiated by relatives, friends or associated criminals. In no case of bribery of a magistrate or prosecutor was any of the four participants personally involved. Three mentioned that prosecutors were bribed by relatives, friends and criminals who robbed with them. The fourth participant said the magistrate accepted a bribe before a bail application was even submitted to the court.

The bribes which corrupt officials received were always monetary in nature. In two instances a vehicle was bought for a police officer. In another, a police officer accepted a house. One participant related: 'I gave him this R50 000. I gave him cars. I gave him the Laser, I gave him the Mercedes-Benz and I gave him the Jetta. I know a lot of things ... his house, where does it come from?'

Ensuring legal representation

All participants had legal representation during their trials, none of which was paid for by the state.

Most of them felt strongly that criminals need legal representatives. Eight of them mentioned that they had attorneys who were always available at short notice. They all said that they paid a monthly amount to a company of attorneys in advance when planning a CIT robbery. Some of the payments were made electronically, and one participant indicated that he had built up a R190 000 balance before using the legal representative's services. Cash payments were also made in advance into the bank account of the attorney's firm.

Four participants mentioned paying cash into the personal accounts of two different legal representatives after their robberies when they became aware that the police were looking for them.

One said if they trust a lawyer enough, they will sometimes phone him beforehand and 'inform him of the job'. Another said: 'You tell a very good lawyer straight away what you did and then he will defend you. But these other lawyers we do not trust.'

From the interviews, it emerged that the robbers mainly used three legal firms for representation. The independent revelations of two participants were worrying because according to them, a legal representative was involved in a CIT robbery. After the interviews, I established that they had both referred to the same attorney.

One participant said that a legal representative – it could not be determined whether he was an attorney or an advocate – was used to convert foreign exchange stolen during a robbery. This legal representative passed away while I was writing this thesis. For the purposes of this research, it is important to directly quote the participant's reply. It lends an additional dimension to the investigation of any CIT robbery. Responding to the question of whether the services of a legal representative are discussed during the planning of a robbery, the participant said:

> His responsibility was to analyse legal issues. And then when it comes to this money, which is difficult to exchange, he was responsible to change those money, especially the foreign currency. It was not difficult for him to change the dollar to the rand or the euro to the rand, and those money was lump sums ... and for a lawyer to go and do that, is not difficult to do so. He was involved from the start until the end.

From their replies, most robbers clearly regarded using a legal representative as important, but they were not unanimous. One participant said: 'Crime money – the only people who benefit from it are lawyers.'

The robbers offered several reasons for using a legal representative:

- To ensure that they get released on bail as soon as possible;
- To prevent them from being exposed to unauthorised interrogation techniques by the police;
- To prevent their self-incriminating evidence exposing them to successful prosecution; and
- To use legal representatives to hide stolen cash.

Case dockets that disappear

One robber was quite convinced that bribing police officials involved with the investigation hampered the administration of justice and police processes. His version of corrupt police officials is supported by several others who said they got information from the police who were part of the investigation. They also claimed they were sometimes notified about planned police arrests and actions against the robbers.

Fourteen participants indicated that case dockets against them disappeared after they had paid for them to disappear. It could not be established where and by whom – police officials, police stations, courts or prosecutors – the dockets were lost. One participant boasted that he succeeded in making all the case dockets against him disappear except the one he was sentenced for and for which he was serving his jail sentence. The people responsible for the disappearance were always remunerated in cash, which varied between R20 000 and R80 000, irrespective of the number of dockets combined in one case. In all cases, the relevant dockets were handed to the robbers. In that way, the robbers were also brought up to date with the investigation and the investigative methods of the police.

The dockets were acquired for three reasons:

- To establish who the witnesses against them were;
- To find out if other members of the group would act as state witnesses; and
- To destroy self-incriminating evidence such as confessions, admissions and other information supplied to the police.

Intimidating witnesses and officials

The participant who boasted of making all but one case docket disappear, mentioned that he had also intimidated witnesses or had them intimidated after becoming aware of evidence filed in the case docket. He also referred to state prosecutors he personally intimidated outside court for hours by threatening them with reprisal. I could not establish whether those threats were carried out. The participant also admitted to having two state witnesses killed and to killing one of his co-robbers whom he had suspected of cooperation with the police.

Despite the comprehensive strategies of thwarting the legal system by bribing police and court officials described in this chapter, justice does catch up with some CIT robbers. Getting caught is the theme of the next chapter.

GETTING CAUGHT

> The last thing was to trust the wrong person. The lady in red. That is my big mistake. ~ Participant 13 (Lochner, 2016)

Some of the robbers thought that they would never be caught. So, when they were sentenced, several suspected they had been betrayed. Eventually, all had to face the consequences of the life they had chosen and the reality of a new future, which is narrated in this chapter.

The participants, discounting those arrested red-handed, had a strong feeling that their girlfriends and wives divulged information to the police about their actions. Most of them felt they erred in trusting their female companions with information that was later used against them.

One thought his companion could not keep a secret, especially under relaxed social circumstances. He said: '*Daar waar hulle drink – hulle praat.* (Where they drink they talk.)'

Another suggested emotions sometimes got out of hand: 'The girlfriend is too close and *as sy kwaad word is dit* revenge (... and when she gets upset, she wreaks revenge.)'

One robber was arrested on the run with his girlfriend. He believed the only person who could have supplied the information about their whereabouts was his girlfriend. He suspects her motive was the reward for his arrest presented in the media. Similarly, a robber found in possession of a stolen vehicle, unrelated to the CIT robbery for which he was serving his sentence, thought his girlfriend was responsible for conveying the information to the police. The source of another participant's problem was less close: 'The last thing was to trust the wrong person. The lady in red. That is my big mistake.'

The mistakes robbers believed they had made which may have led to their arrest make a lengthy list:

- Illegal weapons found in their possession not used to commit crimes;
- Illegal weapons found in their possession used for their crimes;
- Stolen cash found in their possession;
- The group was too large, which compromised control after the crime;
- The selection of the group was inadequate, and information was supplied to the police by one of the group during planning;
- Group members threw money around and it raised suspicion. This led to their arrest whereafter a particular robber and co-robbers were pointed out by those arrested. In most cases, the extravagance occurred in restaurants and bars;
- Younger members of the group publicly boasted of their actions, thereby drawing the attention of the police which resulted in their arrest as accomplices;
- The group's precautions against infiltration were inadequate. The police managed to infiltrate them, which allowed the SAPS to act proactively to catch them red-handed;
- One co-robber revealed some information after the crime and turned state witness. That indicated someone betrayed the group by revealing their identity during the selection of group members;
- While on the run, some of the members panicked and surrendered to the police. According to the participants, this also indicated that the selection of members for the CIT group was not up to scratch; and
- Spirited action by the police and CIT companies was underestimated during the robbery. Consequently, the robbers could not get away as planned.

The participants acknowledged that they made mistakes after their arrest which incriminated them. In particular, they singled out making confessions and admissions or supplying other information to the police. In some cases, those were made by their co-accused, and the police used this information to arrest them. One participant mentioned that he acknowledged his involvement under duress and consequently made a confession after which he was arrested.

Discounting the robbers arrested at the crime scene, 14 of the 18 participants remained on the run until their arrest. Using false identities, they stayed in hotels and townhouses in all the provinces except the Northern Cape. They also used false identities for housing rental contracts. One participant suggested, however, that the muti he used rendered him invisible and that he did not leave his home.

The shortest time any of them hid in a different place was 18 days, the longest being three years. In the latter case, the robber fled the country and became involved in CIT robberies abroad.

Most of the participants found it easy to rent townhouses. The only related problem was convincing the neighbours of their so-called legal work. They regarded the pretence as necessary to prevent the neighbours from becoming suspicious because they did not keep normal business hours. Some of the work pretences they offered were:

- Insurance agent;
- Small business owner;
- Owner of large construction enterprises;
- Taxi owner;
- Bottle store owner; and
- Representative of well-known enterprises.

Two of the participants left the country while on the run. They had no problem clearing the border posts since there is no cooperation between the respective police forces for the extradition of criminals. A news report confirmed the poor policing at South African border posts allows criminals to enter and leave the country unnoticed.[1]

It is significant that 13 of the fleeing CIT robbers at times stayed with trusted family in other provinces. This is contrary to what they themselves believed was the best way to avoid being located.

Participants 2, 3, 4 and 5 were all found guilty of the same two CIT robberies and were tried in a single court case. For the sake of completeness, they were also individually found guilty of other CIT robberies. From the interviews, I gathered that those four, along with other CIT robbers convicted for these two robberies, operated together as a group. Analysing their replies further supported that conclusion.

Only five out of 13 robbers arrested

Transgressors convicted of the same crime get noted in the Correctional Services system as accessories. From the research, I determined that on average five people were found guilty for one CIT robbery. The number of accomplices involved in the robberies in question, based on the information from the participants, averaged 13 per robbery. That meant, judging from this sample, that fewer than half of the group members who participated in CIT robberies were found guilty.

It should be borne in mind that four convicts were found guilty of the same crime. So, the average number of accomplices the participants suggested were used to portray the following exposition. Two participants stated that they were arrested at the scene because of proactive police response and that nine CIT robbers in total were shot dead during the two robberies. That meant that in the case of 15 CIT robberies, 132 robbery accomplices were not arrested.

Table 2. Accused found guilty vs group size during crime

Participant	Co-accused found guilty simultaneously	Actual size of group during crime
1	1	10
2	14	20
3	14	14
4	14	23
5	14	15
6	2	11
7	1	15
8	0	13
9	1	12
10	0	11
11	4	12
12	0	5
13	0	10
14	0	12
15	1	12
16	5	11
17	6	10
18	8	12
Total	85	228
Average	8,95	24

Notes: The more conservative figures were used: Participant 5 indicated that the group was larger without giving a figure. Participant 15 gave a figure of between 12 and 15.
(Source: Lochner, 2016:94)

It was interesting to note that the interviews with participants 2, 3, 4, 5, 16 and 18 revealed that the investigation of their crimes was handled by a team assembled because the events received wide media coverage.

In the case of participant 17, a getaway vehicle broke down and left him stranded. He was arrested shortly afterwards.

Preparing for life after prison

Despite the life sentences served by some, all participants participated in Correctional Services' internal training programmes and declared their interest in training for alternative careers. Some of those destined for release on parole notably underwent skills training to help them get employed or to start a business. Manual skills were mentioned most often, including:

- Electrician;
- Builder or construction worker;
- Carpenter;
- Mechanic; and
- Upholsterer.

Participants interested in studying wanted to use the acquired knowledge to get a job upon release which would enable them to get further in-service training.

Notably, several wanted training as motivational speakers. They wanted to motivate people to steer clear of crime. One wished for a film career; so, he could use his crime career to visually portray the downside of crime. Two others expressed a wish to cooperate with state or semi-state institutions to highlight the detrimental results of crime as a full-time occupation.

One man said: 'Being arrested is ... the main risk. I don't mind dying.'

So, for some robbers, the perceived glamour of taking on the CIT companies and police, spending mega sums of money and living the high life led to wounds or death. For the rest of these participants, it meant being on the run for many months, a drawn-out legal process and eventually many years behind bars. In prison, people introspect themselves and the results of the decisions they made about their lives.

Facing the results of their criminality

Many of them were prepared to supply information about crime once they had been sentenced (see next chapter). The enthusiasm with which one participant was willing to do that, is best described in his own words:

> *Ek het nou warm inligting maar weet nie aan wie om dit te rapporteer nie. Die inligting wat ek het, is oor menslike liggaamsdele wat verkoop word. Mense word verdrink en dan word die liggaamsdele*

> *verkoop.* (I now have hot information, but do not know who to report it to. The information I have is about human body parts being sold. People are drowned and then the body parts are sold.)

The relatives outside remain part of robbers' lives. A participant said: 'One of my daughters are [is] working in Holland and is married to a white man. They will be coming this October to see me. An American.'

Another admitted: 'Next year my grandchildren will be old enough to visit me alone. That is embarrassing.'

A third lamented: 'My children do not respect me. I want to buy my dignity back.'

Despite the unmitigated violence of their criminal careers, imprisonment did give the convicted robbers time to reflect on their criminal careers, as shown in this chapter. During the interviews, they revealed important information for fighting CIT crime. That information is scrutinised in the next chapter.

Note

1. See http://www.netwerk24.com/Nuus/Misdaad/Smokkel-lag-lag-by-Lebombo-as-dit-reen-grenspos-uitdaging-vir-polisie-20150721

ADVICE FROM THE ROBBERS

> He was honest, and I respect him for that … and that is the reason why I will give him information. ~ Participant 12 (Lochner, 2016)

While this research proved that too many robbers and even more robberies and accomplices go unpunished, I believe those numbers would be substantially lower if the results of this research were put to proper use.

The convicted robbers themselves offered hints and information to improve CIT investigations. This chapter will consider such possibilities and emphasise the need for the improvement in the investigation work done by the police and private institutions like the CIT companies. The methods and techniques used by the robbers to spoil or thwart the investigations are also underlined. This will serve to make investigators aware of criminal methods and techniques. So, they are not side-tracked by them.

A question was put to the participants which allowed them to express opinions on where the police could get the best information about the activities of CIT robbery suspects. The suggestions about possible sources of information are discussed in the rest of the chapter.

Public gathering places

All participants recommended shebeens as the place to get information on suspected CIT robbers. They believe that undisciplined robbers spend much money and openly carry and flash around large sums at shebeens. Other social spots were also recommended for enquiries, including discos, sports bars and venues where young people and students, in particular, socialise. Hatfield in Pretoria stood out, but the participants could not remember the other places by name.

One participant mentioned the Waterfront in Cape Town, adding that no one made any enquiries there because so many foreigners visit the place. He thought it would be bad for business if those foreigners noticed the police; so, the police maintain a low profile to prevent international tourists viewing South Africa as a high-risk destination in terms of crime. Other public places mentioned by 13 of the participants were theatres, cinemas, public recreation areas and places where exotic food is made and sold.

Family, friends and the community

Fifteen robbers believed friends and family should be asked about CIT suspects. The girlfriends of the suspects were indicated as the most probable people to supply accurate and complete information to the police. Two robbers believed relatives would divulge information to the police once the media identified the robbers. The conclusion reached is that participants believed the public is expected to reveal information to the police.

Most robbers were convinced that a girlfriend, who for some reason or another is angry with the robber or who has fallen out of favour with him, would be prepared to supply information to the police as an act of revenge. One suggested that girlfriends become used to 'eating money' (in crime parlance spending and having money). For this reason, he believed they would supply information to the police in exchange for a huge monetary reward.

Two participants indicated that the community knew that they were CIT robbers, and one thought that youngsters idealised them. It would be advisable, therefore, for the police to make enquiries within the community, particularly among its younger members. The robbers indicated that the sudden disappearance of well-known CIT robbers from an area for a time would raise suspicion within the community. Such a disappearance could indicate that they had carried out a CIT robbery and that they were on the run to avoid tracing and arrest. It would not be difficult for police intelligence to link their absence to a recent CIT robbery. Participants were also unanimous that enquiries with neighbours or former neighbours of well-known CIT robbers would yield information.

Informers

All robbers mentioned informers as a possible source of information about a CIT robbery suspect. It would appear that all participants harboured an almost irrational fear of the unknown threat an informer represents. The research concluded that they never quite trusted their henchmen and could not be certain of their loyalty. Any among them could be an informer. The importance of informers is illustrated by the suggestion made by one of the robbers. He said a police officer should be required to recruit at least 100 informers before he is allowed to investigate CIT robberies.

Well-known CIT robbers

A participant who has been jailed since the middle of the 1990s raised a strong argument that people held in detention centres should be approached for information. He supported his suggestion by comparing a correctional centre to an ant nest where all the ants gather, and communication with the outside world is easy. Then he mentioned one robber I had interviewed, whom he said had planned and executed several crimes from the correctional service centre. Of his own accord, the participant mentioned several examples of such crimes. I followed up that information and confirmed it to be true.

The robber who organised the crimes from within the jail also confirmed this allegation when I spoke to him during a follow-up interview, without revealing the source of the information. The robber who initially supplied the information was very convinced that he knew what he was talking about. He stated that the correctional facility inmates knew about a robbery and the robbers involved, 30 minutes after the event.

Another participant suggested that well-known CIT robbers who were not in custody be recruited as informers. He believed they had valuable information about other CIT robbers and might reveal information about rival robbers.

Preventative measures for CIT companies

The participants were also asked to make suggestions about the preventive measures CIT companies could put in place to thwart CIT robberies. The question put to the participants was an open-ended one that left room for unlimited opinions. One reply stands out. The participant suggested that security companies need to recruit officials who have the interests of the companies at heart at all times. My conclusion is that they had to be people with integrity. The remaining responses contained many and varied practical suggestions amounting to:

- CIT officials not only require training in handling firearms and the application of security measures, they also need to be physically fit, prepared and trained for greater mental resilience. One participant believed that an overweight CIT official or one with a weak character, would not defend his employer's assets with his life. Participants found guilty of more than one CIT robbery felt that CIT officials were insufficiently trained to combat the new techniques and methods used by robbers;

- CIT officials need to be well paid so that they will decline bribes for information or involvement. One participant expressed disbelief that a CIT official earning R10 000 a month is required to transport R10 million at a time. Four participants questioned the reasons for CIT officials wanting to do such a dangerous job for so little remuneration. The conclusion drawn from this is that the value of the item guarded by the CIT official must have some bearing on his remuneration;
- The screening of officials should be very strict and include psychological evaluation such as psychometric testing. In this way a potential insider could be identified, which may prevent a CIT robbery;
- The number of CIT officials allocated to a vehicle delivering or collecting cash may influence whether it would be attacked or not. This, however, is a consideration only when potential targets are considered and different scenarios are weighed up. However, once a target has been selected because it is deemed to be feasible or profitable, the robbery has been planned and the decision to carry out the robbery has been taken, no security measure would deter the robbers except a visible police presence. By then, the planning is done and the number of CIT officials likely to be on the scene has been considered;
- Modern investigative technology needs to be used. Random lie-detector tests of CIT officials and psychometric evaluation tests to determine their loyalty to their employers were also mooted. All participants who used inside information believed that no robbery could succeed without it. They said that is the very reason why they proposed an effective recruitment and screening process for officials as a measure to prevent CIT robberies. If done during the screening process, they believed this could eliminate potential insider information getting out to robbers;
- An improved location of a CIT company's base was also pointed out as a way of reducing the company's target value. Two participants told how they casually sat at a nearby filling station watching vehicles leaving and returning. Locating the CIT company among other businesses made the surveillance possible without raising suspicion;
- One participant mentioned that company numbers (he called them fleet numbers) displayed on CIT vehicles made it even easier to identify and follow a specific vehicle that, according to available information, may be transporting a large amount of money. He suggested that those numbers be removed;
- The fact that CIT companies take the same routes at the same times to deliver to or collect money from the same premises made planning robberies easier. The participants proposed changing the operation so that robbers would not be able to calculate where and when the vehicle would

be at a specific place, which would complicate the robbery. The participants regarded the unknown as a major deterring factor when considering a robbery. Most of them proposed rotating the CIT officials among different teams because that would eliminate collusion between officials and the possibility of information leaking out;

- Closer liaison between CIT companies and the police. It was suggested that the police be thoroughly informed about the daily operations of the companies. The participants believed that would help the police to carry out visible patrols as a preventative measure on the routes the companies used;
- CIT vehicles be equipped with cameras on the in- and outside relaying live footage to the mother company for instantaneous archiving. That could lead to a quicker response and the footage could be offered as evidence in court. One participant suggested using a satellite connection, saying there was a greater risk of injury to officials should the footage be stored in the vehicle. Robbers would become aware of such footage and do their utmost to destroy or get their hands on it, which would expose officials to greater risk and danger; and
- One participant claimed to have defeated all security measures introduced by the companies to the interior of vehicles. He proposed that companies keep investigating and using new technology, but he did not specify which ones. He also suggested that less money be transported at a time. To me that means the less money transported, the less profitable the target will become for robbers, which implies that they would rather look for more rewarding targets.

Preventative measures for CIT officials

Participants were asked for their opinions on what CIT officials should do to prevent being shot or otherwise injured. All participants agreed that the officials needed to heed orders from the robbers once the vehicle has been forced to a standstill. One suggested that the officials should not try to be heroes. Outside the vehicle, they should equally obey orders and not resist. The very last participant interviewed proposed that the officials not look the robbers in the eye. His reason is that robbers regard that as an effort to identify them later.

Measures for improving crime investigation

Participants made ingenious proposals to this open-ended question, although they may not all be practical or legal. Some suggestions, such as violence, murder, blackmail, abduction, illegal deportation, incitement to commit a crime, torture, illegal bugging, illegal arrest, and illegal confiscation of moving or fixed assets and property, were mentioned but would contravene Section 7 of the Constitution.

Several other aspects relating to insiders were raised. Participants believed all officials should be thoroughly questioned after a CIT robbery because no robbery is possible without inside information, as indicated before. Three indicated that the chances were great that information had been supplied from within the CIT company if no corpse was found at the scene. This means that the chances are slim that CIT officials would be killed when an insider is involved.

All the robbers in the group do not always know the insider's identity. To prevent him being killed, no CIT official would be directly shot at. They were also convinced that the informer would be inside the vehicle or be involved with the delivery or collection of the money, which would render the execution of the robbery or the cooperation of the other officials easier. In such cases, the investigating officials should focus more on the insider's participation in the crime.

Most robbers also pointed out that when an official is wounded superficially (as in the leg or foot) in front of his colleagues, it should serve as an indicator for the investigating officer that he supplied information or otherwise cooperated with the robbers. The insider is wounded to create the impression that he is a victim, and therefore he would not be suspected.

It was suggested that special police units investigate CIT robberies. The rationale for this is that such robberies occur across provincial boundaries. Well-trained investigators who cannot be bribed should be recruited and receive further training to become specialist CIT investigators.

Improved interrogation methods by police investigators were also proposed. This is a sensitive subject participants raised throughout their responses. It appears that the participants experienced police interrogation methods negatively.

All participants expressed the same opinion about the importance of the police using informers. One believed that such informers needed to be used in financial and profile investigations against CIT robbers so that their financial position, including the possession of both moveable and fixed assets, could be determined. He was also convinced that financial and lifestyle audits should be an integral part of all CIT robbery cases, including investigations of the assets of the family and friends of robbers.

For most of the participants, a financial audit means an investigation into fixed and moveable assets in their possession and that a lifestyle audit determines whether they live within their means. Because friends and family are often used to hide stolen money and conceal property or other assets bought with such money, they should also be subjected to investigations.

Nine robbers singled out new technology for the investigation of the crime scene and robbery in general as an important aspect, although they named (as was the case with one participant referred to earlier) no such technology. For most, the compiling of physical evidence was an important aspect, but DNA was singled out. The reason offered was the fact that some of their co-accused in the cases for which they were serving jail sentences as well as others were found guilty based on DNA evidence.

Nine of them were also aware of the evidence value that cellphone technology offers. It was offered as evidence against the accused in five of their trials. I have extensive knowledge of cellphone technology in the investigation of crime. From their responses, I could determine that the participants were not quite on top of cellphone investigation techniques currently used in crime investigation and policing.

Rewards were mentioned as a possible contribution towards the solution of CIT crime. It was suggested that a huge amount of money be offered. One robber mentioned, as pointed out earlier, that the reward offered for his arrest was the possible reason why his girlfriend, with whom he was on the run, may have supplied information to the police, leading to his arrest.

Media use in the investigation of CIT robberies and the tracing of such robbers came strongly to the fore. The mere reporting of incidents in the media did not draw a reaction from the participants. Further aspects did, however:

- Pictures in the media: The display of pictures and the publication of the wanted CIT suspects' identities, be it in print or electronic media, concerned them. Two whose identities were published said nobody wanted his name to be 'dragged through the mud'. Three others pointed out that their wives were unaware of their involvement with CIT robberies. Even before his arrest, one of them was divorced by his wife because of that revelation. It would be safe to argue that, hidden in the responses of both these suspects whose identities were revealed, is a possible method for tracing suspects whose identities are known. From my experience, however, it should be made public only with the greatest circumspection and after thorough planning with all roleplayers in the CIT investigation. In practice, suspects, sometimes accompanied by legal representatives, arrive at investigators' offices or police stations after it has been revealed that they are wanted. In the process, evidence may be destroyed, and it may also influence the interrogation techniques available to an investigation official. One robber said he became more cautious after his involvement in a CIT robbery was exposed in the media. That could complicate tracing a suspect.
- Offering a cash reward: One participant's reaction was that this would cause distrust among CIT robbery accessories. He called it a possible temptation for accomplices to approach the police with information. According to his reasoning, a reward might create the further possibility of the informant revealing information about other crimes (excluding the robbery where the informant was involved) his co-robbers were involved in and about which he had only heard.

- Reporting the amount robbed: This would create suspicion among robbers, especially when the amount each robber gets, does not correspond with the figure mentioned in the report. As pointed out before, the yield is divided equally among the robbers, who know how many participated even though they may not have been present when the money was counted. Because of a robber's suspicion that the rest of the group cheated him, one participant told me that this accomplice supplied information to the police about the rest of the group. He also said that two other accomplices who were involved with him in another CIT robbery (not the one where the informer approached the police) were murdered because they were suspected of stealing some of the money. The one accomplice was deliberately shot and killed in retribution at a subsequent CIT robbery scene by his own group. The participant called this an 'own goal', the football parlance for scoring against your own side. Killing, according to the participant 'was the only option'.

One participant who used to be a police officer offered what he called handy hints for improving CIT robbery investigations:

- The screening of investigators for CIT robberies should be improved and done more thoroughly;
- Any police official spotted near the crime scene and who does not work or live in the vicinity, should immediately be interrogated to determine possible complicity;
- Real efforts should be made by the SAPS to gather more covert information about CIT robberies;
- Police officials driving or owning expensive vehicles (he referred to BMWs and Volkswagen Golfs) should be investigated, since they could only afford them if they earned an additional income; and
- Not everyone should be recruited or used as an informer. His reason was that some robbers pretend to be bona fide informers for the express purpose of supplying false information to the police. In that way, the informer misleads them and creates the opportunity for the robbers to facilitate their planning and acquire information on the investigation of a reported robbery. The planning is made easier because the robbers know in advance what the police plan will be, and how they will operate or react. The robbers are then able to plan around that information.

Conduct against mistrusted accomplices

My experience as an investigator made me realise that it is of utmost importance for any investigator to know that CIT robbers would take violent reprisals against suspected accomplices. This means that officials investigating CIT cases must guard against creating any suspicion because it may cause the death of a suspect. From experience, I also know that accomplices sometimes supply information to the police and that the identity of all informers should always be protected. Section 202 of the Criminal Procedure Act of 1977 makes it compulsory. I regard it as extremely important to point this out.

It is also important to reflect the participants' exact words when referring to informers. It conveys the contempt in which informers are held. The words used by participants were: rat, dog, pig, apartheid scum, *impimpi*, rubbish, pimp, spy, or trap.

In reply to the follow-up question of what happens to a distrusted accomplice, it was stated that such a person would never be part of a CIT robbery again. The fact that he is suspected would be conveyed to other well-known CIT robbers and groups. A meeting would also be scheduled to discuss the fact that the accomplice can no longer be trusted. Besides the other groups being informed, a participant said such an accomplice would be 'punished'. Isolating him from criminal activities and the criminal world must be construed as punishment.

A participant who identified himself as a leader mentioned that a CIT robber suspected of being an informer would be employed in a subsequent robbery in a role where he runs a higher risk of being killed. If the suspect shows any resistance to placement in a high-risk role, he will be regarded with even greater suspicion. Placing someone in a position at the crime scene where he is more likely to be killed is also done to observe the suspect's conduct.

These high-risk positions are usually close to the CIT vehicle and visible to other co-robbers. When the person acts suspiciously by departing from the plan or not following orders, this behaviour increases the suspicion.

A second participant confirmed that a co-robber was killed by other group members 'here where the action takes place' (referring to certain key positions on the crime scene) because he was regarded as a possible spy.

Four participants mentioned that a suspect accomplice would be killed. A participant incriminated himself by admitting that he was responsible for the execution of an accomplice who supplied information to the police. This execution took place after a police official testified during a bail application that the accomplice supplied information to the SAPS.

A second participant expressed his regret about the accomplices he and other CIT robbers had murdered, and he reproached himself for attending their funerals after the murders, the incident briefly referred to earlier. The participant said they were murdered because a police official told the robbers that the victims would be put in a witness protection programme and would subsequently testify against the group.

Knowledge of active free criminals

It was crucial to establish what the participants in this study knew about the criminal activities of well-known CIT robbers and other criminals to determine whether they (the participants) had valuable information. Determining whether they would be able to supply information and to whom, enabled me to make a relevant finding and recommendation on this empirical information.

Replying to the question whether the participants knew of CIT robbers who were free and committing robberies, 13 participants said yes. In response to the question whether they knew of criminals familiar to them who were not in custody (CIT robbers excluded), 17 replied positively. It can, therefore, be stated with some certainty that these CIT robbers were aware of what happened in the criminal community outside the correctional centres.

It was also necessary to determine whether CIT robbers would be prepared to supply information about CIT robberies and or other criminal activities. This would enable the police and CIT company investigators to approach convicted CIT robbers for information at the right time. The first question was to establish whether any information was conveyed to the police during the investigation. The subsequent related questions were asked in the sequence followed in a criminal case during the judicial process. The responses are represented in Table 3.

Table 3. Supplying crime intelligence to the police during the investigation

Response	Number	Percentage
Yes	2	12%
No	16	88%

Clearly, the majority supplied no intelligence to the police during the investigation of the CIT robberies in which they were found guilty. Their response to the follow-up question about the reasons for their refusal is that it was done on legal advice.

The next question, represented in Table 4, was whether they supplied crime intelligence during the trial.

Table 4. Supplying crime information during the trial

Response	Number	Percentage
Yes	1	6%
No	17	94%

Again, most revealed giving no information during their trial, and once again, this was on legal advice.

The final question in the series, represented in Table 5, was whether they would be unwilling to divulge information after sentencing.

Table 5. Unwilling to divulge information after sentencing

Response	Number	Percentage
Yes	1	6%
No	17	94%

In response to this question, only one participant was reluctant to reveal information about criminal activities under any circumstances. He was the oldest of the participants and still denied complicity in the CIT robberies he was found guilty of and for which he was serving a jail sentence.

Various answers were given to the question about who they would be prepared to supply information to. Most felt that it had to be someone trustworthy. Nine participants mentioned more than one person. Eight thought it should not be police officials because they could not be trusted.

Six of the remaining participants, however, said they would supply information to the officers who investigated them. From the response and body language of one participant I observed, I concluded that he had enormous respect for one investigator. His reason was: 'We did argue and fight. I did not plead guilty. He was honest, and I respect him for that ... and that is the reason why I will give him information.'

One participant mentioned that he would rather supply the information anonymously. He was responsible for the death of accomplices and thought there was a possibility of an informer's identity being revealed. He was wary of retribution being taken against his family.

Three participants thought they would supply information to CIT companies, but that it had to be for payment. Another said he would supply information to anyone. Other people or institutions the participants were prepared to supply information to were:

- Business Against Crime;
- The media;
- Political parties and officials;
- Preachers; and
- Church officials other than preachers.

It is important to point out the possibility that after their sentencing, robbers would supply information to the police official who investigated the case against them, on condition they were handled correctly during investigation and trial. Of equally vital importance is taking notice of when a sentenced robber might be prepared to supply crime information. By being aware of these possibilities, police or CIT company officials would be in a better place to approach robbers for information.

It worries me that, according to the participants, no one conducted interviews with them after they started serving their sentences. I believe the crime investigation does not stop once the accused is found guilty and sentenced. Investigation is a ceaseless search for the truth, involving finding out who was responsible for the crime and their motives for doing so. For that very reason, I would have expected that some of the participants would have been approached as part of a process to gain more information about CIT robberies.

At the outset of this research project and based on my own experience, which may also be linked to recent court judgements on corruption, I was thoroughly aware that corruption is an everyday reality. However, I did not know how easily case dockets and their contents disappear.

The reasons CIT robbers offered as to why it was important that those dockets disappeared, raises another important point. This is not only about the destruction of evidence and proof material, but it was also a way to determine at a very early stage whether co-robbers had supplied information to the police. This is done so that the swiftest possible retribution could be taken against co-robbers who had become informers. Such action includes isolating them from the criminal environment, which may be regarded as a punitive measure. The isolation is also aimed at safeguarding CIT robbers as a group and sabotaging the state's case. The action against informers in some instances involves killing them. On this basis, it could be argued that CIT robbers are probably among the most violent of all criminals.

On an almost daily basis commissions of enquiry and other investigations show South Africa to be in the grip of unparalleled corruption. Based on this research, the extent of CIT crime and the penetration of its tentacles into select circles of the South African society should therefore raise further serious concern. The time has arrived not only for the police and legal fraternities to take a hard look at the flaws exposed here. In the current idiom, several other institutions like some casinos, used-car dealers and even sangomas appear to have been 'captured' by criminals.

These are, however, not simply more alarmist revelations. Authorities and a society keen to defeat the scourge of crime will find ample to work with here.

REFERENCES

Axelrod, A. & Antinozzi, G. 2003. *The complete idiot's guide to criminal investigation*. New York: Penguin Group.

Bartol, C.R. & Bartol, A.M. 2014. *Criminal behaviour: A psychological approach*. Essex: Pearson.

Becker, R. 2009. *Criminal investigation*. Boston: Jones and Bartlett.

Bell, W.R. 2002. *Practical criminal investigations in correctional facilities*. London: CRC Press.

Berg, B.L. & Horgan, J.J. 1998. *Criminal investigation*. New York: Glencoe-McGraw-Hill.

Berning, J. & Masiloane, D. 2010. 'The use of modus operandi forms by the South African Police Service to analyse crime.' *Acta Criminologica: Southern African Journal of Criminology*, 25 (1): 84.

Brandl, S.G. 2014. *Criminal investigation*. New York: Sage.

Brown, M.F. 2001. *Criminal investigation: Law and practice*. Boston: Butterworth-Heinemann.

Burger, J. 2015. Senior researcher at the Institute for Security Studies. Speech during a conference on the closing of the specialised units of the SAPS. 18 October 2015. Pretoria.

Businesstech. 2018. 'Private security vs police officers.' Accessed 17 February 2019. https://businesstech.co.za/news/government/251121/private-security-vs-police-officer-numbers-in-south-africa/.

Du Plessis, C. 2015. 'Smokkel lag-lag by Lebombo as dit reën – grenspos "uitdaging" vir polisie.' Netwerk 24. Accessed 18 November 2015. http://www.netwerk24.com/Nuus/Misdaad/Smokkel-lag-lag-by-Lebombo-as-dit-reen-grenspos-uitdaging-vir-polisie-20150721.

eNCA. 2013. 'Senior cops nabbed for cash heist.' South Africa. Accessed 18 July 2014. http://enca.com/south-africa/senior-cops-nabbed-cash-heist.

Fish, J.T., Miller, L.S. & Braswell, M.C. 2014. *Crime scene investigation.* Waltham, USA: Elsevier Inc.

Fosdick, R.B. 1916. 'Modus operandi system in the detection of criminals.' *Journal of Criminal Law and Criminology*, 6 (4): 560–570.

Gilbert, J.N. 2007. *Criminal investigation.* 4th edition. New Jersey: Prentice Hall.

Helfgott, J.B. 2008. *Criminal behaviour: Theories, typologies and criminal justice.* Thousand Oaks: Sage.

Hess, K.L. & Orthman, C.H. 2010. *Criminal investigation.* 9th edition. Mason, OH: Cengage Learning.

IOL News. 2003. 'The anatomy of a cash van heist.'. Accessed 17 February 2019. https://www.iol.co.za/news/south-africa/the-anatomy-of-a-cash-van-heist-114984.

IOL News. 2013. 'Attempted cash heist on N2.' Accessed 15 March 2014. http:www.iol.co.za/news/crime-courts/attempted-cash-heist-on-n2-1.1455794#. VnR7ck3ovlU.

James, S.H. & Nordby, J.J. 2005. *Forensic science: An introduction to scientific and investigative techniques.* 3rd edition. London: Taylor & Francis.

James, S.N., Nordby, J.J. & Bell, S. 2009. *Forensic science: An introduction to scientific and investigative techniques.* 4th edition. London: CRC Press.

Jonckie. 2011. 'Amazing visuals as accident into cash-in-transit vehicle is caught on camera.' Insurance Chat. Accessed 15 August 2014. http://www.insurancechat.co.za/2011-07/amazing-visuals-as-accident-into-cash-in-transit-vehicle-is-caught-on-camera/.

Joubert, C. 2013. *Applied law for police officials.* Cape Town: Juta.

Kenny, J.P. & More, H.W. 2001. *Principles of investigations.* 5th edition. New York: West Publishing Company.

Labuschagne, G. 2015. 'Criminal investigative analysis: An applied perspective.' In *Forensic investigation: Legislative principles and investigative practice*, edited by R.J. Zinn & S.I. Dintwe, 275–304. Cape Town: Juta.

Lochner, H.T. & Zinn, R.J. 2015. *Crime scene investigation.* Cape Town: Juta.

Lochner, H.T. 2016. 'Die gebruik van modus operandi-inligting van gevonnisde kontant-in-transito-rowers in die ondersoek van kontant-in-transito-rowe.' DLitt et Phil thesis, University of South Africa, Pretoria.

Lochner, H.T., Horne, J.S. & van Wyk, M. 2018. 'Die modus operandi profiel van die kontant-in-transitorower as eksklusiewe misdadiger.' *LitNet*, 15 (2): 209–228.

Lochner, H.T., Horne, J.S. & Zinn, R.J. (in press). *Investigation: A comprehensive guide to the basic principles, procedures and forensic processes.* Cape Town: Juta.

Marais, C.W. 1989. 'Die waarde van modus operandi-inligting by die ondersoek van sekere misdade.' *Acta Criminologica*, 2 (2): 46–49.

Marais, C.W. & Van Rooyen, H.J.N. 1990. *Misdaadondersoek.* Pretoria: Henmar.

Maree, A. 2008. 'Armed robbery (bank robbery, ATM attacks and CIT heists) as part of current violent crime in South Africa.' Institute for Strategic Studies. University of Pretoria. August, 26.

McCartney, N. 2008. 'Cash-in-transit robbery.' flickr. Accessed 18 February 2015. https://www.flickr.com/photos/gee-raff/2306784089.

News iAfrica, Sapa. 2010. 'Driver rams getaway car.' Accessed 18 June 2015. http://news.iafrica.com/sa/682221.html.

Osterburg, J.W. & Ward, R.H. 2010. *Criminal investigation. A method to reconstructing the past.* Cincinnati: Anderson.

Palmiotto, M.J. 2004. *Criminal investigation.* Dallas: University Press.

Redrockat, 2012. 'Cash in Transit SBV'. [Video file] Accessed 18 March 2020. *https://www.youtube.com/watch?v=s9YZ1k6sxYw.*

SAPS, 2010. SAPS Annual Report 2010:14. https://www.saps.gov.za/ about/stratframe work/annual_report/2010_22101/8_annual_financial_ statements.pdf.

Scott, J.S. 1978. *Investigative methods.* Reston: Reston Publishing Company.

Sennewald, C.A. 1981. *The process of investigation.* Stoneham: Butterworth-Heinemann.

South Africa. 2000. The Firearms Control Act 60 of 2000. Pretoria: Government Printer.

The Firearms Control Act *see* South Africa. 2000.

Thobane, S. 2014. 'The criminal career of armed robbers with specific reference to cash-in-transit robberies.' MA dissertation, University of South Africa, Pretoria.

Van der Watt, M. 2015. 'The preliminary investigation phase.' In *Forensic investigation: Legislative principles and investigative practice*, edited by R.J. Zinn & S.I. Dintwe, 209–247. Cape Town: Juta.

Viljoen, B. 2015. 'Transitorowers gryp R50 miljoen na skietgeveg, ontploffing.' Netwerk 24, 11 Maart:3

YouTube, 2012. 'The South African Special Task Force Part 1: Doctalen.' (Viewer discretion). [Video file]. Accessed 11 February 2015, but no longer available online. https://www.youtube.com/watch?v=GFqlye79KS0.

Zinn, R.J. 2003. 'Sentenced motor vehicle hijackers imprisoned in Gauteng as a source of crime intelligence.' MTech dissertation, Technikon SA, Florida.

Zinn, R.J. 2007. 'Incarcerated perpetrators of house robberies as a source of crime intelligence.' DLitt et Phil thesis, University of South Africa, Pretoria.

Zinn, R.J. & Dintwe, S.I. 2015. *Forensic investigation: Legislative principles and investigative practice.* Cape Town: Juta.

INDEX

This index is in letter-by-letter alphabetical order; spaces, hyphens and introductory words such as 'and,' 'of,' and 'in' are ignored. A page number in **bold** indicates that information on the topic can be found in a photograph, table or graphic on that page.